Lunch at Delnor

A LOVE STORY

L. HENDRICKS

Lunch at Delnor

ISBN: 979-8-35092-287-5

Contents

1 – INTRODUCTIONS 1

2 – LUNCH 7

3 – THE CONNECTION 15

4 – ONE DAY AT A TIME – RIGHT? 23

5 – THE BIG FIRST STEP – ALMOST. 31

6 – WHEN IS A DATE NOT A DATE? 41

7 – BUCKLE UP! 49

8 – A NEW DAY 59

9 – FAMILY 69

10 – FORE 79

11 – FEEDBACK 87

12 – FEELINGS 91

13 – PILING ON 97

14 – THE HOLIDAY 103

15 – ALONE TIME 109

16 – CRAP 115

17 – THE BATTLE 123

18 – ALL IN 135

19 – THE MERGER 145

20 – LEAVING A MARK 151

1 – INTRODUCTIONS

Delnor Hospital in Geneva, IL is a large modern facility. Actually, it is no longer officially named Delnor since it was purchased by one of the large hospital corporations. However, all of the locals still refer to it as Delnor. As with all modern hospitals, the lobby looks like a resort hotel with large steel and glass framed windows projecting huge amounts of sun light onto the sleek marble and granite floors and counters. The lobby is much larger than a hospital lobby needs to be but provides the feel of luxury and quality that comforts both patients and visitors.

Sitting at the center backside of the lobby is the main reception desk. The reception desk is normally staffed by two attendants whose primary job is to answer questions and provide directions to visitors – plus a few administrative duties. Sitting at the desk today is Rose Hopkins and Belynda Novak. Belynda is a veteran of over 20 years at Delnor – all at the reception desk. Rose, on the other hand, is relatively new and is still in her initial two-week training period.

Janet Davies, the Office Manager, is responsible for both the general office - where they do the payroll and handle patient billings and also the reception desk. There are about 20 people reporting to Janet, including all of the reception desk attendants. Janet leans heavily on Belynda to manage the reception desk. Although Rose reports to Janet on the Org. Chart – she takes her day-to-day direction from Belynda.

Everyone knows Belynda, she has become one of the faces of Delnor and is looked upon as one of the old timers who can answer any question and knows how things are supposed to work.

Rose on the other hand, came to Delnor with no hospital or receptionist experience. Delnor had attempted to recruit an experienced receptionist but after 3 months with no response to their recruitment ads, they decided to hire Rose. While Rose did not have hospital or receptionist experience, she is a college graduate and has spent the last ten years with a local CPA firm as an office manager and Jack of all trades. It was a good job that paid much more than she was now making at Delnor. However, the hours at the CPA firm were long and Rose was a salary worker so she wasn't paid for the overtime. In addition, that job came with pressure – especially during tax season – which Rose didn't want anymore.

Rose had recently turned 65, went on Medicare and was ready to slow down a little. She wanted a job with normal hours and less stress. She wanted to leave her job at work and not have to think about what she had to get done tomorrow. She was willing to give up some amount of compensation to get this easier and less stressful life. She took a fairly large reduction in income in the job change from office manager to receptionist. She had also taken a fair amount of heat from friends and family about making this change but she didn't care – it was what she wanted.

In addition, she had recently gotten divorced and sold the home where she had lived for the last 30 years and raised her children. She then moved into a new apartment and as such, had a little nest egg and didn't have to deal with all of the home ownership headaches and expenses.

Now in her second week of training under Belynda, things were going very well. She was over the normal new job anxiety. In Rose's case, the anxiety was a little greater than normal. The lack of hospital experience had concerned her and the fact that she was African American, made her a little concerned about how she would be accepted and treated. The area around the hospital in Kane County was predominately a white conservative and upper middleclass area. The CPA firm where Rose had previously worked was also predominately white but somehow the hospital seemed different and a little intimidating.

Two things that Rose had going for her was her intelligence and her looks. She had a college business degree and was very attractive and looked 55 instead of her actual age of 65. At five feet seven inches tall, she had a very stately figure. After her divorce and the sale of her home, she was financially independent and secure. She knew that she would be fine, even if this job didn't work out. Her friends constantly told her that she should be looking for a rich husband as she was a great catch for some man.

Most people visiting a patient at Delnor would naturally come to the reception desk to ask what room a patient was in – even if they already knew. Of course, everything was computerized and she would simply enter the patient's last name into her computer screen and the room number would appear. If there were any visitor restrictions limiting access to the floor, room or patient, they would also appear on the screen. She would then direct the visitor to the correct elevator.

Her other task was to monitor access to the cancer treatment facility. The doors to that facility were located directly behind the reception desk. There was a large sign in front of the doors to the cancer center that read NO AMITTANCE – Authorized Medical Personnel Only - All other visitors may register at the reception desk. The cancer treatment facility had controlled access due to the type of treatments being administered – like radiation. Also, because of the weak immune system of some of the patients – they couldn't be exposed potential germs or infections. All visitors had to be pre-approved by a cancer doctor and even then - had to pass through a second control point inside of those outer doors. The second control point would double check the visitor but also then make sure that they were appropriately dressed or masked and covered for the visit.

Two people could normally handle the traffic at the main reception desk. There were times in the morning and immediately after lunch, when things got crazy busy – otherwise – it was a fairly low stress job.

This being Rose's second week of training, she was still paired with Belynda. Belynda was the most experienced attendant and trained all of the new attendant hires. After her training ended, Rose would be placed on rotating shifts along with the 6 other attendants on staff. The desk was staffed 24 – 7 except that there was just one attendant on 2nd and 3rd shifts. Some were full time, like Rose – meaning that they were looking for 40 hours a week, while others were part time, looking for around 20 hours a week.

It was Thursday of Rose's second week of training. She was feeling pretty good about the job, the people she had met and thought she had made the right decision in leaving the higher stress world of public accounting.

Just then she noticed an older gentleman wearing a mask and baseball hat walking toward the reception desk. She was ready expecting him to stop ask for directions or a patient room number. But he didn't stop. He just waved to Rose with his left hand as he walked past reception on the right side heading directly toward the cancer center doors and the NO ADMITTANCE sign.

Rose moved toward the CC doors – "can I help you?" No answer from the gentleman as he kept moving. Now much louder and authoritatively – "CAN I HELP YOU SIR?"

The man stopped in his tracks and pivoted toward Rose and began walking slowly toward her.

"I don't think so." The man replied.

"Well - you can't enter the CC without signing in at this desk and getting approval."

"Really, you must be Rose."

"Yes - how did you know that?"

"I work here – well not work exactly but I volunteer here at the CC and I was told that there was a new receptionist and that her name was Rose. My name is Bill – Bill Campbell, like the soup."

"That's great but do you have some kind of identification?"

"I do." Just as Bill was reaching into his wallet to pull out his hospital ID card, Belynda walked over.

"Hey Bill - how are you doing?"

"Great, just about to show Rose my ID."

"Bill – you don't need to do that."

"Rose – this is Bill Campbell and he is a full-time volunteer at the CC and has access without checking in at the desk."

"Bill, where have you been? I haven't seen you in a while."

"I've been kind of busy in the CC and up on 5 – mostly coming and going in the nights and evenings."

The 5th floor was where the ICU was located and the rooms for the cancer surgery patients

"OK well have a good day." Belynda stated.

"Thanks Belynda - and Rose, good to meet you."

"Same to you Bill." Rose replied.

As Bill returned to his path toward the CC doors, he stopped and turned and said in a loud direct voice – "Hey Rose – maybe I will see you at lunch today."

"OK, Rose replied." She was not sure why or where they would meet for lunch.

Belynda was still standing there after Bill departed through the CC doors. "Rose, sorry about not telling you about Bill. He normally comes by every day – it's odd that it has been almost two weeks since I have seen him."

Rose asked – "what is up with Bill, what does he do in the CC."

"It's a long story". As Belynda was about to tell Rose about Bill, several visitors approached the desk and had to be helped.

After they departed, Rose asked again – "what's the story with Bill?"

"Oh right – well his wife was in the CC about a year or more ago – maybe two years now – time flies. During her time here, he never left her side – I mean almost never. You would be surprised how special and unusual that is. Anyway, she passed – hey, her name was Rose also. After she passed, Bill just kept coming in. The staff didn't know what to do with him at first and almost had to have security remove him at one point. But Bill just started spending time with patients that didn't have anyone with them to support them or to provide comfort."

"That is amazing," Rose noted.

"Yes, it is. Sometimes he just sits with out-patients getting treatment and sometimes he goes up to the cancer ward and sits with the more serious cases. Some are children and some are adults. He often gets hooked with a particular patient and stays with them for days at a time without going home. However long that lasts, he is back the next day. He hasn't missed a day since his wife passed."

"Wow – amazing." That was the only thing Rose could think to say.

"Yes – a special guy but not a young man. It has to be taking a toll on him."

Rose asked – "how old is he and what was that comment about lunch?"

"Oh – I think he is around 70, maybe a little older. Regarding lunch, he sometimes takes lunch around noon and if we are in there at the same time, he will sit with us for a few minutes. It's rare that he is there and never stays for more than a few minutes. Turkey sandwich and Pepsi – that's it."

Rose and Belynda returned to their reception desk duties for the remainder of the day. Rose made a mental note about Bill and his comment about meeting her for lunch. It was getting close to quitting time and things were pretty quiet at the desk. As such, her mind began to wander. Tomorrow is Friday and her two-week training period would be over. Would she still be paired with Belynda next week or would she be assigned with someone else that she didn't know? As a number of unrelated random thoughts began running through her mind, she was startled by Belynda.

"Goodnight Rose. See you in the morning"

"Goodnight Belynda. Thanks for your help today."

Rose then gathered her things and headed for her car as the 2nd shift receptionist arrived and took over the reception desk.

2 – LUNCH

A Few Weeks Later –

In the weeks since meeting Bill, Rose had seen him a few times as he entered the CC area, but had never seen him leave. He always said good morning and asked how she was doing. However, she had not run into him in the cafeteria during her lunch break as he had mentioned when they first met. As such, she had pretty much forgotten about the lunch comment - until today.

Rose settled into her 9 to 5 shift, five days a week. Normally, she worked Monday through Friday with Belynda. At times she worked the occasional weekend or 3nd shift – when she was asked to fill in for somebody. She was an empty nester as both her children were grown, so working one weekend a month was not a problem. Also, it meant some extra money for her. In her previous job, weekends were normal and she didn't get paid OT for the weekend hours.

The scheduled lunch time or allowed lunch time was 45 minutes, which she normally took at noon. She had thought that she would eventually meet some people to have lunch with but that hasn't happened. Since the other receptionist has to be at the reception desk while she was at lunch, she normally ate alone.

Like all larger organizations, there were natural cliques that existed. At Delnor, you would see the medical personnel (doctors and nurses), the office personnel (accountants and clerical personnel) and the support staff (maintenance and janitorial) all eating together in separate groups. There were always also a fair number of patient visitors spread throughout the cafeteria – sometimes eating or grabbing a snack or drink or just using it as a place to get away and relax.

The cafeteria at Delnor was exceptional. It was a large clean and bright space and like the lobby had the modern feel of a resort with the stainless steel and granite counters. They had a variety of choices from soups and salads to full meals and deserts and everything was fresh and of good quality. The cafeteria was also very clean and well maintained and it was obvious that the hospital felt that a good cafeteria for the staff and guests was important. There was always a chef or cook on duty and other cafeteria staff willing to assist and provide something special if requested. Also, and not a small point, the prices were very reasonable. This was important to Rose given her new lower earnings.

She had fallen into the routine of grabbing a soup and/or salad for lunch and eating while she read a book. Recently, she had gotten hooked on the Michael Connelly books – Harry Bosch and Renee Ballard – along with a few of the Micky Haller character books. She had always been a book reader and her recent attraction to the Michel Connelly books was started when – at her daughter's suggestion – she started watching Bosch on Prime TV. She watched the entire seven seasons twice - as she thought it was about the best show she had ever seen.

Today, Rose was enjoying some chicken noodle soup and a small chopped salad and was about half way through the "Dark Sacred Night" a Ballard and Bosch novel by Michael Connelly. She was startled when someone put down a cafeteria tray directly across from her at the four-seat table where she was sitting. She didn't recognize the man now sitting down across from her.

"Hey Rose, how are you doing?"

"I am sorry, do I know you?"

"Kind of – I am Bill Campbell. We met a couple of weeks ago in lobby." It took Rose a few seconds as she had never seen Bill without a mask and without a baseball cap. Normally a Cubs hat or a golf hat. Rose had noticed the Cubs hat as she was also a life-long Cubs fan.

"Hello, she said with some hesitation. I did not recognize you are first. I haven't seen you without the face mask and without your hat."

"That's right – I didn't think about that." Bill replied. "Well now you know – some facial hair and very little hair on top. A family curse on my mother's side. The head not the goatee."

"You look fine. Not sure what I was expecting but I think a little different. Have you always had the goatee?"

"No – it is a Covid thing. When that whole thing started, I just felt like doing something different. I had a mustache in the 70's but nothing since then."

"I think the goatee looks good. It provides good balance with the head thing."

"Head thing? You mean being bald?"

"Yes – looks good with the bald thing. Didn't want to say bald – some guys are sensitive about that."

"I am not – it is what it is. Don't let me stop you from eating your soup and salad. The chicken soup is one of my favorites – I get it a lot."

"But not today?"

"No – I went with the exciting turkey sandwich and chips today. Needed something more solid than soup."

Rose spoke up after a brief pause. "So, it has been a while since we first met. You said that you would see me at lunch and that was several weeks ago."

"I know, sorry about that. I normally always eat lunch but it seems that it is rarely at noon. I work irregular hours and often the nurses have lunch brought up to me from the cafeteria or somewhere else, depending on the time of day."

"What is it exactly that you do in the CC – is that what you call it?"

"Yes, the CC?"

"What is it that you do there?" Rose having to repeat the question.

"Not much really. I just help the nurses and spend some time with the patients. I see that you are reading a Harry Bosch book, really a Michael Connelly book." Bill obviously trying to change the subject.

"Yes – I loved the TV show so I started reading the books and love them as well."

"Me too." Bill replied. "I think that I have read most of the books and watched the TV show several times."

"Same here. When there is nothing on TV that I want to watch, I go to Prime and replay the best episodes. Using the Apple controller - you can fast forward to the best parts."

"That is amazing, I do the same thing Rose. I often go to episode 10 of each season and replay that episode. Those are normally the best and most dramatic episodes."

The two of them then engaged in a lengthy discussion about the various Bosch episodes, the plots and characters, etc. Suddenly, Rose's phone buzzed. It was a text from Belynda asking where she was as it was one o'clock and she was now 15 minutes past due in getting back to the reception desk.

"Crap – I am late. I have to get back - Belynda is texting me. Sorry but I have to run."

As Rose got up, she noticed that she had not eaten any of her soup or salad – virtually nothing since Bill sat down about 45 minutes ago.

"Rose – tell Belynda that it is my fault. I talked your ears off and delayed you getting back. In fact, I will stop by and talk to her to explain when I am done."

Rose then noticed that Bill hadn't touch his lunch either.

"OK Bill, see you around. Maybe tomorrow."

"I hope so." Bill said, as Rose hustled back to the reception area.

Belynda was waiting for Rose when she returned. She was not angry, just a little annoyed and worried. Rose had never been late before in returning from lunch. In fact, she rarely took the entire 45 minutes, let alone an hour and 15 minutes as she had taken today.

"Sorry Belynda, I just lost track of time." Rose said.

Belynda replied. "That Bosch book must be really interesting."

"No, I hardly even read my book. Bill finally joined me for lunch. We were talking about Bosch, he is also big fan of the show and I just lost track of the time."

"OK – no problem. I am glad the two of you finally connected. He is a fascinating guy. Not bad looking either – right?"

"No, he is not. But it is not like that – just two people talking."

"Right, well that is good as you would be public enemy number one with many of the other ladies around here if the two of you connected."

"What do you mean?"

"Can't explain now, I have to go get something to eat and thanks to you – my time is short." Belynda then headed to the cafeteria.

When Belynda got to the cafeteria Bill was gone. However, as she was going through the line, she got bombarded with questions from several of the lunch ladies about Bill and Rose being so engrossed in conversation during lunch. It was very unusual to see Bill sit down to eat – especially for that long. They had noticed that he didn't eat his lunch until after Rose departed.

Belynda played dumb and pretended not to know anything about it. However, she was thinking two things – how catty people can be and whether there could be something brewing between Bill & Rose.

When Belynda returned to the receptionist desk things were very busy. People were lined up in front of Rose - so Belynda jumped in and one long line became two long-lines. They were experiencing the early afternoon rush. People normally visit their friends and relatives in a hospital first thing in the morning or immediately after lunch. So, Belynda and Rose were used to handling the post lunch crowd but today was little heavier than normal. They were very busy until about 4:30 and there had been no chance to continue their earlier discussion.

At almost exactly 4:30 they both looked up and the lobby was empty. Each took a deep breath and a seat in their raised bar stool style chairs. No sooner had they sat down and took a deep breath – Rose turned to Belynda and asked about her earlier comment.

"What did you mean that I would be public enemy number one?"

"What – oh nothing – sorry, I shouldn't have said that."

"No. Belynda, I want to know. What is it? The black / white thing?"

"Oh God no." Belynda replied. "Look – It has been around two years since Bill's wife died. A lot of people have gotten to know him and realized what a great guy – remarkable guy really - that he is. It also doesn't hurt that he is attractive and supposedly is fairly well off. Anyway, several of the unattached ladies – around his age – have attempted to connect with him over lunch, have asked him over for dinner, have invited him to parties, etc. But Bill has said no to all of them or sometimes, that he would think about it and then just not show for the party."

Belynda paused for a second and then continued. "Nobody has had a lunch with him like you did today. So, that is something different and people noticed. Some people will be naturally jealous or curious."

"What do you mean – who noticed?"

"I can't say but a couple of people mentioned it to me this afternoon. I told them that they were crazy and that it was simply lunch. You can easily guess who would have asked me about it."

Rose assumed it was the cafeteria crews who had commented to Belynda as they were constantly looking over at her and Bill during lunch.

"That's nuts." Rose stated. "It was one lunch for an hour – wow – people are crazy."

No sooner had the words left Rose's mouth then a voice jumped in from the left side of the desk. "Who's crazy?" Bill was asking.

"Nobody." Rose replied. "Just people in general."

"How true that is." Said Bill. "I am heading out – see you ladies tomorrow. Rose, I really enjoyed lunch today. Let's do it again tomorrow. Wait!

Sorry, tomorrow's Saturday. Let's do it again on Monday." Bill then headed out toward the parking garage.

Rose watched him as he was walking across the lobby to the exit. He looked fairly tall – at least 6 feet – had broad shoulders and an athletic type walk. He definitely had a spare tire but he carried it well.

Rose could feel Belynda's eyes on the back of her head. She turned to looked at Belynda and noticed that Belynda had a big grin on her face and was nodding as if saying – I knew it.

"Stop it." Rose said.

3 – THE CONNECTION

Rose had a good weekend. She saw both of her children and baby sat for her 13-year-old grandson - Jordan. She was able to relax a little and read a little Bosch. She did some grocery shopping and even went to the show with her friend Gloria. Gloria's nickname was GG because her last name was Grant. It was Roses first visit to the theater since the Covid shutdown. Her children had been telling her to see the new Spiderman movie - so that is what they saw. Neither of them understood what all the fuss was about – assumed it was more for younger people.

In spite of this busy weekend, the whole Bill situation kept popping into her mind. There was really nothing to be concerned about, who cares what people think or say. In spite of telling herself this, she kept thinking about it and didn't understand why. She thought about mentioning it to Gloria but decided not to as she didn't want GG thinking that she was somehow having a thing with or interested in a guy at work. Then it would definitely become a big deal.

Rose had been married to the same man for 32 years. It was an OK marriage but far from a perfect marriage. She met Carl – her ex-husband - in college and dated him for about 3 years before getting married. They had met in her first accounting course. Both were going part time to Elgin Community College – a local Junior College. Rose finished the two-year program – although it took three years because she was also working full time while attending school. Rose earned BS in Business from Northern Illinois University three years later. Again, working pretty much full time while finishing the last two years. Carl quit after one year and took a job at a local electrical contracting firm.

The good part of the marriage were the two children – Robert and Stephanie. Both were good students and both college graduates – due in large part to Rose's efforts. The tough part of the marriage was Carl's roving eye. Their marriage endured several separations due to Carl's infidelity. For the sake of the children, Rose would always take him back after having kicked him out. However, when Carl pulled one of his stunts yet again after the children were out of the house and on their own – Rose was done. She changed the locks and called a lawyer and got a divorce. It was a tough time for Rose and hard on the children as well. The final step was selling their home, splitting the proceeds with Carl and moving into her new apartment.

Rose loved her new apartment. It was brand-new and she was the first tenant. Everything in the apartment complex was clean and modern. She even bought new furniture instead of taking her old worn stuff from the house. She was on the top – 4th floor. There was an elevator and she had a bright sunny view. As they say, she felt like she had a new lease on life.

The new job in concert with her new apartment made her feel like everything was perfect or at least going really well. However, she kept thinking about what Belynda had said. She didn't want to be public enemy number one at her new job. The answer was simple - she had to avoid Bill. That should put an end to that issue.

Monday started off as normal. Belynda was off this week so Rose was paired with Katie - who used to work at the desk but had recently taken a position in the hospital accounting office because it paid a little more. In fact, Rose was hired because Katie had made the change from receptionist to accounting clerk. Katie was now the primary back-up for the reception desk for vacations, illnesses, days-off, etc.

Rose had decided to bring her own lunch today and eat in the general office conference room in order to avoid any continuation of the whole Bill thing. That eliminated any potential anxiety she would have about lunch.

It was a busy morning. Mornings were always their busiest time and Mondays were always their busiest day. It was a typical busy Monday morning. There was not much down time or idle time for conversation with Katie – which was OK as Rose didn't really know her. She had only been briefly introduced to her on her first day.

Things finally settled down a little about 10 AM and Rose noticed Bill walking in from the parking garage and then across the lobby heading toward the CC doors behind her desk. She thought about acting like she was busy and didn't notice him but it was too late – they had made eye contact.

"Good morning, Rose. Good morning, Katie." Bill stated in a loud and pleasant tone.

Both replied back to Bill with a Good Morning.

Rose thought she had dodged a bullet as Bill passed without mentioning lunch. Then he stopped just outside the CC doors and walked a few steps back toward the desk.

"Rose – see you for lunch at Noon?"

"Yes – I will be there." She replied.

As soon as Bill departed, she immediately said "what the heck" - to herself. Before she could figure out why she had agreed to lunch after bringing her own, she could feel Katie's eyes on the back of her head. She hesitated for a second and then slowly turned toward Katie, hoping she was just being paranoid. Katie was looking at Rose and had that same big grin on her face that Belynda had last week.

The rest of the morning, Rose must have checked the time about 100 times. She couldn't get a handle on what she was feeling. At times she was dreading sitting down with Bill again because of the high school type gossip it was creating but also felt a school girl type excitement about it. She hadn't felt that way about a boy or man in a long time.

At Noon, she grabbed her brown bag lunch that she had brought from home. As she was walking to the cafeteria, she thought that it might look bad for her to bring a lunch into the cafeteria and not buy anything from them. As she was about to walk through the cafeteria door, she tossed the lunch into the trash can.

As soon as she entered, Rose looked to the right where her and Bill had sat last week. He was already there with his lunch reading a book. He waved to her and she proceeded through the cafeteria line getting her normal soup and salad. Today the special was vegetable soup, so she got that with a small chopped salad.

When she got to where Bill was sitting and exchanged hellos – everything changed. The anxiety was gone as soon as they stated talking.

She noticed that Bill had the same Turkey sandwich as before and had brought a Michael Connelly book.

"Another, Bosch book?" Rose asked. "I thought that you had read them all?"

"Well, after saying that last week, I went on-line and checked. I have not read them all. Connelly has written about 35 books and I have read only about 16. So, I was able to find a couple of his older books over the weekend. I finished another one last night so I am just starting this one."

"Which one did you finish last night?"

"The Black Box – it was good but must have been one of the earlier ones. I probably should be reading them in order but it doesn't seem to matter – they all are good."

The conversation went on as they talked more about Bosch, what they did over the weekend – especially Rose's trip to the show to see Spiderman (Bill hadn't seen it yet) and her time with her children.

The mentioning of her children opened the door for the exchange of personal information which had not happened yet.

"Rose – tell me about your children." Bill asked.

Rose replied. "I have two. Robert who is 36 and an architect and Stephanie who is 34 and is the manager at the Hallmark store in Geneva Commons."

"Really, I have been in there several times and probably have seen and maybe even talked to her. Are they married?"

"Robert is not – unfortunately, but Stephane is with two children. She and her husband Eddie have a son – Jordan – who is 13 and a girl Kelly who is 10."

"Wow – congrats, that is great."

Rose asked. "What about you? Do you have any grandchildren?"

"No – not yet. I have two sons Matthew and David. Matthew is 37 and married and works downtown Chicago in advertising. He lives in Hinsdale. David my youngest is 34 and is an accountant with Culligan. He is not married and lives in Schaumburg. I have kind of given up on grandchildren – it doesn't look like it is going to happen."

"Oh, you never know." Rose replied.

She hesitated for a second thinking about how to phrase her next question. "I heard that your wife passed away a couple of years ago?"

"Yes – not quite two years yet. She got sick about four years ago – cancer – and fought it for a long time and then passed right here at Delnor. I guess that is why I work or volunteer here."

Rose could see Bill's demeanor change and eyes sadden when talking about his wife. It was obviously still hard for him to talk about it so she decided to change the subject. "Bill what is it exactly that you do here in the CC?"

"Wait, before I answer that – what about your husband?"

"We divorced about two years ago. He was a ladies' man and I should have kicked him out long before that and I would have if it wasn't for the kids. We haven't spoken or seen each other much since the divorce and that is a good thing."

"OK – what I do here at Delnor? Not much really."

"You, said that the last time I asked you. I hear differently from Belynda."

"Well - I spend time with patients getting treatment in the CC. I look for those patients who are especially nervous or scared or don't appear to have much family support. I also spend time up in the CC ward with those patients getting surgery – again looking for those in special need of support."

"Is it a 9 to 5 thing?" Rose asked.

"No – I usually come in every day just to see what is going on and what is needed. Sometimes I have to stay a little after 5 or come in whenever help is needed."

"How do you know when help is needed?"

"Sometimes, they call me or sometimes I just read the patients eyes."

"Who calls you?"

"The nurses at either the CC out-patient desk or the nurses upstairs in the CC ward."

"How many days a week are you here?"

"Almost every day – just depends on what is going on."

"Wow, that is an amazing commitment – almost every day and on a volunteer basis! That has to be hard on you?"

"I don't mind, I have the time and I don't sleep much."

"How could you? Does the hospital pay you?

"No. I don't expect them to. I just come in because I want to help and I don't expect them to pay me. I am sure that someday soon it will end and I will move on to something else."

Just then, Rose's phone buzzed – a Text message form Katie – "Need some help at the desk."

"Ah crap." Rose noticed it was 1:15 and she had done it again. "I can't believe this, I am late again. Bill – if we are going to keep having lunch, I need to set my alarm and be back on time."

"OK got it." Bill replied. "I will talk to Katie and explain."

"No – no need for that. That will only make it worse."

"Well - I definitely want to have lunch with you again." Bill stated.

The directness of Bill's words got Rose's attention. "So do I." She replied.

"OK Rose, have a good afternoon – see you tomorrow, if not before."

As Rose was cleaning up her area and leaving, she noticed that just like last week, she had not touched her lunch. Yikes she thought. Made one lunch and bought another and didn't eat either. Whatever this is with Bill is good for my diet.

When she got back to the reception desk Katie was waiting with that exasperated look on her face. "I know, I know – I am sorry. It will never happen again."

"OK". Katie simply replied. She then headed out for the cafeteria and her lunch. Rose noticed an aggravated tone in her voice but hoped it was nothing serious.

Things got busy for Rose in the afternoon rush so she didn't have time to dwell on Bill, being late or the potential for another round of gossip around their extended lunch.

When Katie returned from lunch she seemed in a better mood and seemed to have settled down. She jumped in and helped Rose handle the remaining afternoon visitors. Rose couldn't help herself – asking Katie "if the cafeteria ladies were talking about her and Bill again."

"Oh yeah." Katie replied. "I got an earful. They have the two of you dating, living together or married."

"Oh my God. This place is a real Peyton Place."

Katie asked, "what is a Peyton Place?"

"You don't know that expression?"

"No."

Rose had to explain about the 1960's TV show that led to the expression.

"Oh well, it is what it is. Two lunches shouldn't be such a big deal." Rose noted.

"I agree. I think it is more about Bill. Several ladies have tried to engage him or get close to him with no luck. You come in and in your first month, you seem to have made a connection. That is going to get noticed."

"I know – I heard the same thing from Belynda – but noticed by whom?"

"The ladies in CC and up in the CC ward. They are a close-knit group. They have gotten close to Bill over the last couple of years and really are protective of him and think a lot of him. They have invited him to numerous events parties, dinners, etc. Bill has even said that he would come but never has. While he is the nicest guy you would want to meet – he has kept his distance on a personal level."

"OK – good to know." Rose said. "I am not going to worry about it anymore. It is what it is – only two lunches. I will take it a day at a time."

The rest of the day was uneventful at the reception desk. In fact, things got so slow that Katie asked Rose if she was OK with her leaving a little early today. Rose had no problem with that so Katie left for home at about 4PM. Rose thought that she might see Bill but there was no sign of him. The 2nd shift receptionist arrived a little early so Rose headed home at about 4:45PM.

4 – ONE DAY AT A TIME – RIGHT?

Tuesday morning arrived and Rose was back at the Delnor reception desk with Katie – who was still filling in for Belynda.

After telling herself that she wasn't going to worry about the rumor mill and what people thought – that is exactly what she had thought about all of Monday night. She couldn't believe that after having only two lunches with someone, people were freaking out. It was like being back in high school.

She couldn't help wonder if race and class were playing a factor. Would people be reacting the same if she was white? Were Bills' protectors not only guarding against her as the wily female looking to get her hooks into him, but also because she was black and just a receptionist and not a nurse or professional like the ladies in the CC?

Rose decided not to bring her lunch today. If Bill wanted to have lunch, that is what she was going to do and the heck with what anyone thought. Also, she had effectively purchased two lunches yesterday and not eaten either one – she can't afford to keep doing that.

Just then she spotted Bill heading her way across the lobby. It looked like he was dressed for golf with a Calloway hat and golf vest over a polo shirt. He looked a little more dressed up today.

“Morning Rose, Morning Katie.” He stated loud enough for both to hear. This time he stopped in front of Rose. “Lunch today?”

“Yes, that would be nice.” Rose replied.

Great and off he went through the CC doors.

As noon approached, Rose began to clear up her area and prepare to head over to the cafeteria. Katie noticed and said, “have a good lunch – see you at 12:45 right?”

“Yes – I will not be late – I promise.” Rose replied.

Rose passed through the cafeteria doorway and immediately looked to the right but Bill was not there. She stopped and looked around and could not see him anywhere. He must be running late she thought. So, she got her lunch and sat in their normal spot, waiting for him to arrive. She had not brought her book so after about 20 minutes, she was done with her food. She waited another 10 minutes in case he showed – but he didn't. She cleaned up her area and was back at the reception desk by 12:40 – five minutes early.

While she was eating lunch by herself today, she noticed that she was being observed by the lunch ladies – as they were known. She could almost see the smirk on their faces when Bill failed to show.

Katie noticed the time when Rose returned to the desk. “Wow, a quick lunch today. Did you guys run out of things to talk about?”

“No, he didn't show.” Rose replied.

“You were stood up on your third date?” The sarcasm irritated Rose a little but she let it pass.

“Did he even text you saying that he wasn't coming?” Katie asked.

“No – but I don't think that he has my cell number. No big deal anyway. Have a good lunch.” Rose said to Katie, hoping to end the discussion.

The rest of Tuesday was uneventful with no appearance by Bill. Rose was thinking that Bill not showing was just like what Katie and others had mentioned about him blowing people off or not showing up after saying that he would attend some event. Maybe that is just his M.O. vs getting close to someone.

This feeling was reinforced on Wednesday when there was no sign of Bill at all. Rose didn't seem him in the lobby and he was MIA for lunch in the cafeteria. This time though Rose had brought her book and made progress on the latest Michael Connelly, Bosch book.

It did begin to feel odd as he had said that he works every day and now all of a sudden – no sign of him. Did something happen? Again, a good part of her evening was spent thinking about Bill.

Thursday began with the normal morning rush. Again, no sign of Bill and this time Rose hadn't noticed until about 10 AM – which she took as a good sign.

About that time, Janet came by and dropped off the Quarterly Newsletter. Both Rose and Katie stopped what they were doing and looked at Janet as she piled about 100 Newsletters on the reception desk. There was an awkward moment of silence as Janet looked back at them without saying anything. Janet finally spoke up. "Ladies please keep about 20 copies on the reception desk for people to take as they desire. Come see me if you need more. Also, someone needs to put 5 in every waiting room on each floor and/or ward. Please do it today – OK?" Janet did not wait for a response.

This was all new to Rose as a quarterly newsletter had not been issued since she started at Delnor. Katie mentioned that she would distribute the newsletters to the waiting rooms, but Rose jumped in and asked if she could please do it. Since Rose had not met many people and hadn't really seen much of the hospital, she thought that this would be a perfect chance to change that. Katie agreed, saying – "knock yourself out. Call if you get lost."

Rose grabbed a stack of about 20 newsletters as that was about all she could carry at one time.

She started with the CC directly behind the reception desk. She got stopped like everyone else at the inside CC desk. Luckily, she knew the person manning that desk today.

"Hi Julie – here to drop off the March quarterly newsletter." Rose stated.

"OK Rose – you need to put a mask on. Leave a few newsletters in this small lobby and then I will buzz you in." Julie replied.

Rose did as Julie suggested. After getting buzzed in Julie asked – "have you been in the CC before?"

"No – is there another visitor room in here?"

"Yes, to the right – first door on the left."

Rose followed her directions and found a small room that was empty with a love seat, two chairs and an end table. There were some old magazines already piled on the end table. She put the newsletters on top of the magazines.

As she was re-tracing her steps to leave, she noticed the nurses stand. She looked around but no sign of Bill. She approached the nurse on duty to introduce herself.

"Hi, I am Rose from reception."

"Wow – Rose – I have heard a lot about you. It is good to meet you. My name is Gina and this is Megan." Gina pointed to the nurse at the desk behind her. Megan was on the phone and waved with her left hand.

"How can I help you Rose?"

"Oh, I am just dropping off the March newsletter in the waiting rooms. Would you like one?"

"Yes – I will take one for Megan as well. Hey, as a new employee, your picture should be in here."

"Really – I haven't even looked at it yet." Rose set down the stack of newsletters that she was carrying and started to page through the newsletter. Sure enough, there was a section about new employees with her picture and a brief bio. "Great, I hate that picture." She said out loud.

Gina heard her and smiled as she was answering the phone. Rose picked up the stack of newsletters that she had set down and waved to Gina and started to leave. She was about half way to the door when she stopped and took one last look around wondering if Bill was there.

"He's not here." Rose turned around to see who was talking to her – it was Gina.

"Who's not here?" Rose asked.

"Bill – he is up on 5." Gina smiled and returned to her phone call.

Rose decided not to engage with Gina and simply said "OK – Thanks."

Rose headed back out to the main lobby and walked over to the elevators. She started up floor by floor hitting each visitor area and also asking the nurses if they wanted one. She found out later that each hospital employee was mailed one to their home so she didn't need to worry about giving them one. Janet hadn't mentioned that. By the third floor she was out of newsletters. She headed back down to the reception desk and grabbed another arm full of copies.

By the time she got to the 5th floor, she was exhausted. She again had to make her way through a floor reception area because it was a cancer ward and it was also the intensive care ward. This reception desk was manned by Gabrielle – who Rose was meeting for the first time. After getting past the reception desk, she found the waiting area on her own as she had figured out that each floor had the same basic layout.

After dropping off some newsletters in the waiting room, she started heading back to the exit. She paused briefly with a thought of looking for Bill but there was definitely a different feel to this floor because of the Intensive Care rooms – more quiet and more medical staff moving about. As such, walking around looking for someone didn't feel appropriate.

Rose stopped at the 5th floor reception desk to say goodbye. Gabrielle asked if Rose knew that there were two waiting areas on the 5th floor?

"No, I didn't know that. I got the one down the right hallway. Where is the other one?"

The one to the right is the Intensive Care room. There is also a cancer ward waiting room down the left hallway.

"OK Thanks." Rose replied and headed that way.

She found the room and was surprised when she found Bill sitting alone in the room. He looked horrible. He stood up as soon as Rose walked in and seemed relieved to see her. Rose approached him and noticed his eyes – both drained from no sleep and red from what she guessed was crying. She couldn't help herself, she set down the newsletters and put her arms around him to give him a badly needed hug. He hugged her back and they just stood there not saying a word. She could feel his shoulders slump and relax into her arms. A feeling came over Rose that she hadn't felt in some time.

At that time a nurse walked in –

"Bill, I am sorry to interrupt but the Joneses are here looking you."

With that a young couple walked in. They were only in their late 20's to early 30's. Both the husband and wife had the same exhausted look like Bill – with red eyes from crying. The wife walked directly up to Bill put her arms around him and started crying saying thank you – thank you, over and over again. The husband joined them in a group hug all three crying.

Rose was now standing back giving them their space. The emotion on display was overwhelming to Rose, not really understanding what was going on and why Bill was involved. She had tears rolling down her cheeks from just watching this scene play out. She then noticed a nurse standing outside the doorway who was motioning to Rose to join her and leave the small waiting room.

Rose did as the nurse asked and left the waiting room. The nurse then approached Rose and put her arm around her and asked if she was OK. Rose answered yes and asked the nurse what was happening?

The nurse explained that the couple's 3-year-old son had died today. Bill had been with the boy and the parents since Tuesday. The couple had two other kids so were in and out but Bill never left his side.

But that was three days ago, Rose noted. You mean that he has been here all that time?

"That's right." The nurse answered. "That is just what he does."

"Oh my God." Was all that Rose could say.

With that, the couple exited the room. They thanked the nurse and headed out. Rose quickly headed back to the waiting room to check on

Bill. As she entered Bill was wiping his eyes and attempting to pull himself together when he noticed Rose.

"Hey, thank you for coming. I am sorry that you had to see that."

"Don't you apologize for that. That was the most amazing thing that I have ever seen. What you did for that couple is a miracle. You need to get home and get some sleep."

"Yes, I do. I also need a shower as I am pretty ripe."

Bill asked, are you heading back down to reception?

"Yes." Rose replied.

"OK – let me grab my stuff and I will go down with you."

Bill headed out of the waiting room and Rose grabbed the unused newsletters to take down with her. She met up with Bill at the nurse's station. He had a small bag and jacket Each of the three nurses on duty came out from their desks and gave Bill a hug and kiss and thank you. It was amazing for Rose to see. Each also told him to sleep in tomorrow or take the day off and get some rest.

Rose and Bill rode down to the 1st floor together without talking. Rose was kind of overwhelmed by what she had witnessed and just wasn't sure what to say. As they got to the front desk, Rose set the newsletters on the desk and turned to say goodbye to Bill and was surprised that he was right next to her and leaned in for another hug. He thanked her again and said that he would see her tomorrow.

Like the nurses, Rose suggested that he take a day off. Bill replied OK – see you at 12 tomorrow for lunch.

As Bill started to leave Rose called out to him.

"Wait." She walked up to him with her cell phone in her hand. "What is your cell number?"

Bill gave it to her and she immediately dialed it on her phone. Rose heard Bill's phone buzzing and said – "don't answer that. Now you have my number and I have yours. Text me if you need anything."

"OK – Thanks I will."

When Rose got back to the desk, she realized that it was after 5 and Katie was gone and the 2nd shift attendant was now on duty. Gary was the attendant – someone else she had not met before. She introduced herself as Gary asked where she had been. Passing out the newsletters she noted.

Rose grabbed her stuff and headed home. She was emotionally spent and couldn't imagine what Bill was feeling like.

Thursday night was a strange night for Rose. She felt very sad for what she had witnessed with the young couple and what they had gone through. It made her cry when she thought about it.

She also reminded herself that she took this job to have less stress and pressure – what a joke. In 10 years at the CPA firm, she never had an emotional day like today.

At the same time, her thoughts also kept going back to Bill. The hug had been something special to her and she thought to Bill as well – at least she hoped so. She hadn't had romantic feelings about a man since her divorce and even long before that, because of the issues with her ex-husband. This was a little new and exciting. She didn't want to get ahead of herself as she didn't know what Bill was feeling about her. He had lost his wife and seemed to be avoiding any relationships – at least according to the hospital staff. Maybe he just needed a friend and wasn't ready or didn't want a romantic relationship?

At that time, she heard her phone buzzing in the other room – a text message. She didn't recognize the number immediately and then realized it was from Bill.

"Hey, thanks again for being there today. It meant a lot to me that you were there. Look forward to seeing you tomorrow. Bill"

Rose replied. "No problem, I look forward to seeing you as well. Goodnight."

A big smile appeared on Rose's face.

5 – THE BIG FIRST STEP – ALMOST.

TGIF was definitely the theme at Delnor each Friday. Today was no exception. Everyone was always a little happier and friendly knowing that there was no work tomorrow. For those who were scheduled to work Saturday, definitely a little less energy.

Rose was a little early today. The 3rd shift attendant was still on duty and there was 20 minutes before her shift started. As such, she decided to run to the cafeteria for a coffee and donut. The morning coffee was free in the cafeteria – a nice perk supplied by the hospital.

As soon as she entered the cafeteria - she noticed Bill sitting in his usual spot. Instead of heading to the coffee table, she walked over to Bill.

"Hey, thought you were going to sleep in today?"

"Yeah, that was the plan but I don't sleep much. I was going to go hit some golf balls before coming in but then it started to rain. So, I decided to get some breakfast."

"I didn't know that you were a golfer?"

"I use to play a lot but haven't played much recently. I been thinking about getting back into it for some physical activity."

"OK – I have to get to the desk. Still on for lunch?"

"Yes, we are – see you at 12."

"OK, Rose replied." She then headed off quickly to the reception desk.

It was a normal morning rush at the front desk. It was Katie's last day for filling in for Belynda. She was looking forward to getting back to her regular office job. Dealing with people on a daily basis when you are not use to it can be exhausting.

Things slowed down about 11:30 and Rose started organizing her area thinking about leaving promptly for lunch. Just then she noticed Janet heading their way.

"Rose – thanks for distributing the newsletters yesterday, Janet stated. I heard you had some excitement on the 5th floor? Excitement is probably not the right word."

Rose knew Katie was just a few feet away and was taking this all in.

"Yes – it was something different, unexpected and caught me off guard."

With that, Katie jumped in. "What happened?

Rose responded. "A young couple's son had died and they were there thanking the nurses.

For some reason, Rose didn't mention Bill, probably because she didn't want to add fuel to the gossip mill fire.

Janet noted. "Just so you know, the nurses are required to document patient and family interactions like that for the insurance record – just in case. That is how I heard about the incident. The nurses said that you handled yourself very well."

"OK – Thanks." Rose replied.

"Rose – I know that you are heading for lunch. When you are done, can you please stop by my office. Nothing bad – just have something for you. It will only take 5 minutes."

"But I have to get back so Katie can take her lunch at 12:45."

"I am sure that Katie doesn't mind waiting 5 or 10 minutes. Right, Katie?"

"Not a problem." Katie replied. Rose wasn't sure that Katie really meant that but Janet wasn't really giving her any choice but to agree.

Janet walked back toward her office. Rose immediately turned to Katie. "What is that all about?"

"I have no idea. What the heck happened up on 5 yesterday?"

"Just what I said. It was a very emotional scene with a lot of crying and Bill was in the middle of it."

"In a good way?"

"Yes – the couple had come back to thank Bill as he had been with their son for three days without leaving. I just happened to be talking to Bill when the couple arrived. It was very emotional, like I said."

Rose noticed the desk clock read 12:03 – Crap – I have to go.

"Say Hi to Bill."

"I will." Rose replied – not even worrying anymore about who knew or what they thought.

Bill was in his usual spot when Rose entered. She headed directly to the food line and got her usual soup and salad – chicken noodle and Caesar salad.

She put down her tray across from Bill. She took out her cell phone and placed it next to her tray so she wouldn't lose track of the time and be late again.

Rose asked. "No turkey sandwich today?"

"No, decided to get wild and have the chicken nuggets."

"Well, I am trying the Caesar salad for the first time."

"How boring must our lives be if our excitement is our lunch choices?"

"I just had some excitement. Janet stopped by the desk to thank me for handing out the newsletters yesterday. By the way, that is why I was up on 5 and ran into you."

"Oh – OK – I didn't know why you were there but I was glad you were. Well, that was nice of her to stop and thank you."

"She also mentioned the whole incident with the couple stopping by. She said that the nurses record the incident for insurance purposes and that is how she knew about it. Did you know that?"

"Yes, at the end of each shift, the head nurse has to complete a write-up of any unusual patient or family interactions. It is so the hospital has a record to refer to in case there is a lawsuit down the road. You know, nurses leave and people forget what happened and the lawsuit can be years later."

"OK – that makes sense. Janet said that the nurses were complimentary about me."

"Well, that is a good thing."

"Yes, but then Janet asked that I stop by her office after lunch. What is that all about?"

"She didn't say why?"

"No, just that it was nothing bad and would only take 5 to 10 minutes."

"Well, I wouldn't worry about it – probably nothing."

For the first time, both Bill and Rose were eating as they talked. That helped make it a more normal and relaxing lunch. Rose decided not to dig deeper what had happened yesterday, she figured that Bill didn't want to re-live that emotional incident. She did quiz Bill a little more about his family, golf and favorite restaurants in the area.

Rose looked at her phone and noted that it was 12:40.

"I have to get going. I don't want to be late for my meeting with Janet."

As she was getting up and picking up her tray Bill stood up. "Don't worry about your tray. I will return it."

"Are your sure, I can do it."

"No – I've got it." Bill said.

"OK – Thanks, I appreciate that."

"Hey, let me know how the meeting goes."

"OK – I will text you."

So, Rose headed over to Janet's office which was in the general administrative wing on the first floor. Rose had been in there a couple of times for interviews before she was hired and on her first day. She had to fill out the new employee paperwork. However, she had never been in Janet's office.

When she arrived, Janet was in her office and her door was open. Rose knocked gently on her door frame ask if she was ready for her.

"Yes, please come in." Janet replied.

Janet asked Rose to have a seat at a small conference table in her office. Janet took a seat next to Rose and turned sideways in her chair facing toward Rose.

"Thanks for coming Rose." Janet stated.

"No problem." Rose replied.

"First let me start by saying that we are very happy with your work performance. I think you have been here about four weeks – right?"

"Yes, I think that is correct."

"Well, we have had nothing but very positive reports and feedback on you. So, from the hospital's perspective, we are very satisfied with your performance."

"Thanks – that is good to hear."

"Also – as I mentioned earlier, the head nurse on 5 was complimentary about how you handled yourself yesterday. I have been involved in those type of circumstances and I know that they can be very stressful. How are you doing after seeing something like that? Did you take it home with you?"

"Yes. I thought a lot about what happened last night. I felt really bad for that young couple."

"That's natural. You know we have people available for you to talk to if that would help."

"You mean psychologists?"

"Yes, or other medical professionals if you would like."

"No, I don't think I need that. I should be fine."

"OK – well they are available at no cost to you, if you want to talk to someone about what you are feeling. It is part of the hospital EAP – Employee Assistance Program – at no cost to the employee."

Janet continued. "Rose, the emotional impact from an experience like this can be days or weeks after the incident and normally appears as depression or sadness. So, be aware if you experience or feel anything like that."

"Janet, thanks - I will keep that in mind." Rose replied.

"The last thing that I need to talk about Rose is Bill Campbell."

"Bill? What about Bill?"

"Well Rose – I hear things. You know how that works. I just am looking out for you and Bill. We live in a different world today."

Rose was surprised and not sure how to respond or what to say – so she didn't respond. She was waiting to see where Janet went with the topic next.

"Look Rose, there is no rule against you dating Bill. Also, it's none of my business. However, I just want you – and Bill – to know that whatever happens will be noticed and talked about around the hospital. I assume that you saw yesterday how special Bill is. The staff thinks a lot about him and are very protective of him. I just wanted you to be aware."

Again, Rose did not respond immediately trying to gather her thoughts.

"Thanks Janet. Just so you know, Bill and I are not dating. We are friends and have lunch together most days. I am not even sure how that started. However, I do think a lot about him and think that he is a really great guy. I didn't really understand what he did here until yesterday."

Rose paused for a moment before continuing her response to Janet. She wasn't sure that she should be saying this to her supervisor but then decided - what the heck – and continued.

"Janet – one more thing. Bill is not a young man. The hours and days and stress that he is putting in without going home is not healthy for him. If something happens to him because of his schedule, it could be a problem for the hospital."

Now Janet paused a little before responding – looking unsure about what to say.

"Rose, I think that is a good point and thank you for bringing it up. I will give that some thought and discuss it with the medical staff."

You're welcome, Rose responded. Rose had a little bit of panic set in as she realized that she may have said something inappropriate. Maybe something that Janet would mention to the nurses that would come back to bite Rose in the butt.

"OK, Rose – keep up the good work. Please keep the EAP in mind."

"I will - thanks."

With that, Rose started back to the reception desk. She looked at her phone and saw that it was 1:30. Yikes, she thought, Katie is going to be upset. Sure enough, Rose got the death stare from Katie.

After apologizing, she told Katie to go to lunch and she jumped in to handle the after-lunch rush – which, thankfully was a little less than normal.

When Katie returned, she had again calmed down. She immediately asked what Janet had wanted. Rose decided not to say anything about the Bill discussion – thinking that would only add to the rumor mill.

"Nothing really – she just wanted me to know that the EAP program was available if I needed it after yesterdays' experience."

"Oh." Katie stated, sounding a little disappointed that it wasn't something juicier. "That was nice of her."

Rose noticed it was a little after 4 PM and she was ready to go home but had to wait till 5. Her phone buzzed and it was a text from Bill.

"How did the meeting go?"

Rose now had to think about whether she should tell Bill about their discussion about him. She didn't want to create a problem or friction between Bill and the hospital. She also didn't want to lie to Bill.

Rose texted back. "The meeting went fine. No big deal as you thought."

She figured if he asked her a direct question about the discussion, that she would reply honestly.

Another buzz – Bill again – OK good. "I will meet you at 5 and walk out with you."

"OK – sounds good." Rose replied.

Sure enough, at exactly 5, Bill was there.

"Ready - he said?"

"Yes absolutely." Rose replied.

She was happy to be heading home. It had been two stressful days in a row and she took this job because she wanted less stress. The thought of pouring a glass of wine, putting on her sweats and sitting down in front of the TV seemed like heaven.

As they were walking to the garage, Rose asked. "So, any plans this weekend?"

"No, nothing, how about you?"

"No nothing really. I hope to see my grandchildren and spend a little time with them at some point."

"That sounds good."

"Hey Rose, since neither of us have plans, would you be interested in having dinner tomorrow night?"

Rose stopped in her tracks and turned to face Bill. "Really – you mean like a date?"

"No not like a date - a date!"

"Yes – Yes – I would like that."

"Great – pick you up about 6?"

"Yes – that's fine."

"OK – I need your address. Text it to me when you get a chance."

"Will do."

"Any preferences on locations or food?"

"No whatever you want is fine."

"OK – I am looking forward to it. See you tomorrow."

Rose replied. "OK."

Bill went one way to his car and Rose head the other way to hers. After she got into her car, she immediately thought about what she had said to Janet – we're not dating – right?

6 – WHEN IS A DATE NOT A DATE?

So much for her thoughts about relaxing and watching TV on a Friday night. Now Rose had to decide what to wear, should she get her hair done, what were they going to talk about on the date and who was she going to call tonight to tell.

First, she had to text Bill her address. This was a little more complicated than normal as she was in a large apartment complex with many separate buildings. She sent him the address with some directions and ended with - call or text when you get here and I will come down.

She decided to call GG first as her daughter would be dealing with her kids on a Friday night. GG answered but said that she was at dinner with her husband and would call her back. Crap – Rose thought. I have big news and nobody to tell.

With time to kill, she decided to check Bill out on the internet. She was surprised that she had not done this before now and knew that this would be the first thing that others would do. There was a lot out there about Bill, especially on LinkedIn. He is a CPA and has an MBA. He was a CFO, then President of several companies and Chairman of 3 different companies. Over the last 20 years he had been working for a Cleveland based private equity company. Rose thought a very impressive career and immediately wondered whether she was a good match or had enough in common with him.

She then googled Rose Campbell, Bill's wife. Her obituary popped up with all of the normal family info that Bill had mentioned. No picture of her or job background on LinkedIn.

The phone buzzed and it was GG returning her call. They exchanged some small talk about their week, where GG went for dinner and what she ate before Rose mentioned that she had news.

"What is it?" GG asked.

"I have a date tomorrow night." GG let loose with a loud shriek! It's about time she yelled.

Rose could hear GG's husband in the background asking what was wrong. Nothing GG told him – Rose has a date. About time – she could her husband say.

"Who is it?" GG asked.

"A guy from the hospital."

"What's his name?"

"Bill"

"Is he a doctor? That would be great if you got yourself a doctor."

"No – he is a volunteer."

"What – a volunteer? You mean he doesn't get paid. That's OK, he must be rich."

"I don't know but I don't think so."

"Where does he live?"

"In St. Charles."

"He's rich. Probably one of those big houses off of Randall Rd. You know with the big lots."

"I am not sure where he lives exactly but I think it is in St. Charles."

"What is his name?"

"Bill"

"Bill what?"

"Campbell"

Rose could then hear GG typing on her computer.

"OMG – the Bill Campbell who is president and chairman and all that stuff?"

"Yes, I think so."

"What do you mean you think so?"

"Well, I have only known him a few weeks and haven't hired a private detective yet to check him out." Rose said sarcastically.

"Very funny – is this guy white?"

"Yes, he is." Another shriek by GG. Again, Rose could hear GG's husband asking what? Rose is dating a white man. Big mistake – Rose could hear her husband say.

"How did you know he was white?"

"Rose – not many brothers in St. Charles, with these job titles."

"What does he do at the hospital?"

"I told you volunteer work."

"What type of volunteer work?"

"He spends time with cancer patients – sits with them. His wife died of cancer at the hospital a couple of years ago."

"Did you know her name was Rose also?"

"Yes – how did you know that?"

"Everything is on line, girl."

"Is he cute?"

"Yes, he is good looking – bald with goatee and about 70 – I think."

"Bald? I wonder if the equipment still works?"

"GG stop it."

"OK – where are you going tomorrow?"

"Just dinner and I do not know where yet."

"Oh – if he buys you dinner, you have to sleep with him, girl."

"GG"

"Just kidding – but second date for sure. What are you going to wear?"

"Not sure – I have been thinking about that."

Make sure it is sexy – show off the goods.

"GG, I have to go. I have to call Stephanie. I will talk to you tomorrow before I go out."

"OK - I will talk to you. Henry is calling me anyway. He wants to watch some dumb movie. Bye."

"Bye."

Rose looked at the time and it was after 9. It should be safe to call her daughter now. She called her daughter expecting the same reaction that she got from GG.

"Hey Mama – how are you doing?"

"Great – just calling to check in and see how things are going."

"Things are good. Just watching TV with the family and relaxing for the first time today."

"What's new with you – how is the job going?"

"Real good. In fact, I have a date tomorrow night with someone from work."

Again, a loud shriek into the phone. The next five minutes were a repeat of the GG call with her daughter's husband asking what was wrong and the daughter having to explain. However, her daughter's reaction to the news that Bill was white was not the same as GG. She got quiet and more serious causing Rose to ask what was wrong?

"Mama, I just don't want you to get hurt. There are still a lot of issues with Black/White couples dating. Have you guys talked about this?"

"No, it never came up. He is a really special guy and I don't think it is an issue for him."

"Mama, it is always an issue. It sounds like you are hooked on him already?"

"Maybe a little. We had some shared experiences at the hospital that kind of brought us together."

"What shared experiences?"

"Work stuff – emotional experiences around the death of a child. That kind of stuff."

"Mama – you're a receptionist. How did you get involved in something like that?"

"Because of him." Rose told her daughter the story and how it affected her.

The daughter was stunned.

"Mama, you should have called me the day it happened. Are you sure that you are not just awed by what he does and not by who he is?"

Rose's response was immediate. "No – I felt the connection long before this incident. That just confirmed to me who he is."

"OK – Mama. Have you told Robert yet?"

"No. I was thinking about waiting until after tomorrow night. If the date doesn't go well, no need to get him fired up."

"OK – what about politics – have you talked politics with him yet?"

"No – it never came up."

"What if he is a conservative – a Trump guy?"

"One step at a time Stephanie. Let me get through tomorrow night and then I will worry about all the other stuff."

"OK – I am going to stop by tomorrow - if that is OK."

"Yes, absolutely but not too late as I will be getting ready."

"OK – I may come by Monday morning also, while you are at work. Probably around 9 or so after I drop the kids off at school. I need to use your printer."

Rose had been given a color printer by her son which she never used. She wanted Stephanie to take it but she hadn't so far.

"Stephanie, you need to just take the printer. I never use it."

"OK, next time I am there with Eddie, we will take it."

"OK – see you tomorrow."

"Bye Mama."

Rose looked at the time and it was 10:30 PM. That went better than expected. No glass of wine, she was exhausted and needed to get some sleep. As she laid in bed, thoughts about the date rolled around in her mind. All the things that GG and Stephanie had mentioned – the black/white thing, politics, Bill's education and background, etc., etc. Also, she felt guilty about not telling her son, but then she was out.

Rose woke up to a beautiful sunny Saturday morning. Saturday was her normal food shopping and dry-cleaning drop-off day. In spite of her anticipation for the date with Bill she wanted to keep her normal routine as opposed to sitting around and thinking about things.

She ran to her local food store – the Jewel – which was literally 5 minutes away. The dry cleaner was in the same strip mall so she dropped off some cleaning and picked up the clothes that she dropped off last week.

By the time that she got home and put away the groceries, her daughter texted that she was there and on-her-way up. Rose had given Stephanie a key so she didn't need to let her into the building. Something else that Rose liked about this new apartment complex, there was excellent security. No more buzzing people in – you needed an electronic key fab to enter the building and a separate key fab to enter the apartment. So, security was aware of visitors coming and going. Also, no delivery guys – all packages had to be delivered to the rental office.

Stephanie arrived with Jordan and he was happy to see grandma. Rose made them both lunch. As they ate lunch, Rose quizzed Jordan about school which she knew he hated but she was concerned about his low grades. She knew that he was a smart kid but just didn't like school and she worried that he may not want to go to college or have the grades to get into college.

Stephanie asked several questions of Rose about Bill and the date to get her mom off of the Jordan school discussion. This was the first that Jordan had heard about his grandma going on a date - which he couldn't believe. This allowed Jordan to turn the tables and quiz his grandmother which Stephanie enjoyed seeing.

Rose's phone buzzed as Stephanie and Jordan were questioning her about the date. It was a text from Bill.

"Rose, really sorry but I have to cancel our plans for this evening. I got hung up at the hospital. I will try to call you later. Bill"

The surprise and disappointment must have registered on Rose's face as her daughter immediately asked – "Mama, what is wrong?"

"Well, my date just cancelled."

"What – why?"

"He says that he is hung-up at the hospital."

"On a Saturday? That sounds suspicious. What the hell does hung up mean?"

"I guess it means that he went in today and is sitting with a patient and feels that he can't leave."

"Can't you call him?"

"No, I am not going to call him. He cancelled. It is up to him to call me."

"Well, I don't want you to be alone tonight. You come over for dinner."

"Thanks Steph, but I need a night to just relax and watch some TV. It has been a really crazy week. I thought that you guys had plans anyway?"

"We do, but nothing we can't cancel."

"No - you go – I will be fine. I will see you at church in the morning."

"OK Mama – call if you need anything."

"I will, thanks. I love you."

"Love you too, Mama."

As the door closed and Rose was alone, she could feel the disappointment flood over her. She thought to herself – now I need the EAP!

7 – BUCKLE UP!

Rose was glad to see Sunday morning arrive. Saturday night had been tough on her. She read a little Bosch and watched some Bosch on Prime. She tried what Bill had mentioned, replaying episode #10 of each season and using the Apple controller to fast forward through the boring parts. That worked and ate up some time but brought her thoughts back to Bill.

She couldn't help think about what others had told her about Bill agreeing to go somewhere and then either not showing up or cancelling. Just like he did last night. Maybe he is just not ready to have a relationship and the hospital thing was just an excuse. Or – maybe there are other issues – race, politics and all the other stuff that Stephanie and GG had mentioned. He never texted or called last night or this morning as he said that he would try to do. The more she thought about it, the more depressed she got. She really liked him and hated to see it end before they even got started.

She made it to church by 10 for the morning service. She tried to clear her mind but she knew it would be difficult as she would see Stephanie and GG and maybe Robert at church. Robert was more of a C & E church goer so she would likely not see her son – which provided some relief as she had not told him about her date.

After church, she had to relive the whole Saturday night date cancellation episode with GG. GG called it worse than being stood-up which

Rose disputed. She also told Rose to write him off and find a nice doctor at the hospital to marry. Rose mostly listened and let her have her say before heading home. Stephanie was mostly quiet and supportive not wanting to pile on to what GG was saying. Although, Rose could see some agreement in Stephanie's eyes when GG advised her to "dump his ass".

Rose was driving back to her apartment after church and started thinking about going to the hospital to see if Bill was there. So, she started to head toward the hospital while debating with herself if she should go there or not. What was she hoping to accomplish? What does it mean if he is there or if he is not there? How is she going to know if he is there or not – look for his car, text him or just go up to the 5th floor? Would it seem like she didn't believe him or that she was checking up on him – what would be her excuse for being there at all?

As the debate rolled on in her mind – Rose realized that she was pulling into the hospital parking garage. She then realized that she was not even sure what kind of car Bill drove. She thought that she had seen him walk to a large SUV the day when they walked out together but she wasn't sure of the make or color. This is nuts she thought.

She parked her car and decided she would go in to the reception desk and pretend that she was looking for her Michael Connelly book. She had to think for minute about which one she was reading – The Crossing.

As Rose approached the reception desk - she wasn't sure that she would even know the receptionist on duty as she had not met all of the weekend crew yet. Lucky for her, Gary was on duty again.

"Rose, how are you doing? What are you doing here on a Sunday?"

"I can't find a book that I was reading and thought maybe that I left it here Friday."

"I haven't seen any books laying around. What did it look like?"

"Kind of brown – it has Michael Connelly in large letters written across the cover."

"No – sorry, I haven't seen it."

"No problem – it was a long shot. So, anything going on here - any activity?"

"No, all is quiet – which is great."

"Seen anyone walking around?"

"Like who?"

"Just people – like Janet, Belynda, Bill?"

"No but I think Bill is here."

"Why do you think that?"

"The sign in sheet from last night had a delivery from Potbelly for the 5th floor. That usually means Bill is here. That is his favorite."

"Ok, thanks." Rose replied. Trying to act like she wasn't really interested. "I am out of here and heading home."

"OK – take care Rose."

Rose started walking back toward the parking garage. She stopped as she was passing the elevator lobby. Another internal debate had begun – should I go up to 5 and see if he is there? She would not have the phony baloney excuse this time to explain why she was there. It would look bad if she just showed up looking for Bill. Easy answer – she couldn't do it. But she could stall a little and visit the cafeteria, just in case Bill was there.

She started for the cafeteria, unfortunately she had to pass by the reception desk again. Gary was still there. "Now what Rose?"

"Oh, I just decided to grab a cup of coffee." She kept moving not wanting to engage in a lengthy conversation. She got her coffee and looked around – there were a few people, likely family of patients but no Bill.

OK – time to go she told herself. She headed back to the parking garage – having to awkwardly pass by Gary for a third time – this time she just smiled. She didn't stop by the elevators but just made quick time for the parking garage. She entered the garage trying to remember where she parked when her phone buzzed.

It was a text from Bill. "How are you doing? Just finished up at Delnor."

Rose decided to get in her car and start moving as she didn't want to run into Bill at the hospital. She didn't want him to know she was checking on him. She got in her car, started the engine and hooked up her phone so she could drive and text via voice command. She replied to Bill when she was a few blocks away from the hospital and heading home.

"Just finished running some errands and heading home. Is everything OK?"

"Yes – just wondering if you were interested in getting together this afternoon or tonight."

Rose hesitated thinking about how to respond. This made her feel much better that she hadn't been stood up and that he had been at the hospital but she wasn't sure if she wanted to go through the whole date thing again. So, she decided to get the lay of the land before responding.

"How long have you been at the hospital? When did you go in – Saturday afternoon?"

"No – Friday night."

"Since Friday night – without going home?"

"Yes."

"You must be exhausted?"

"Yes, a little tired, but as I told you I don't sleep much."

"Bill – why don't you just come here to my apartment? I will make you a late lunch or early dinner. Then you can get home early and get a good nights' sleep."

"Rose, I don't want to put you out. We can go out, I will be fine."

"No – you are coming here - end of story. We don't need the hassle of going out. You have my address, right?"

"Yes – just leaving the hospital now, being there in 15 or so. We can also do take-out if that would be easier.?

"No, I will make us something. See you soon. Thanks."

Rose was just pulling into her parking spot in front of her building. She quickly headed upstairs. Her place is always neat and clean but she wanted to pick-up and straighten up a few things before Bill arrived. She also had to check her freezer and fridge to see what she could make Bill to eat. She didn't want to do take out for her first meal with him. She remembered that she had made beef soup the other night hoping her son would come over this weekend as it was his favorite. That was perfect as she made a good beef soup and it would be quick to heat up. She only had to cook the noodles.

Her phone buzzed with a text from Bill. "I am here at the building door."

"OK – be right down."

Rose grabbed her key fabs and headed down. She always took the elevator as her place was on the 4th floor. As she entered the building lobby, she could see Bill through the door window. She opened the door and immediately noticed that same exhausted look on his face of someone who hasn't slept in a couple of days.

She greeted him with a hug saying welcome, it is good to see you. He hugged her back and gave her a kiss on the cheek saying that it was good to see her as well. Rose made a mental note that the cheek kiss was something new.

They got to Rose's apartment and she immediately gave him the quick tour.

"Rose, this is very nice. I could get use to this. Wow – what a great view."

"Not much to see but a good view."

"Yes, it is. Rose, I want to apologize for last night."

"You don't need to apologize, things happen and you had to help."

"Yes, I do. I could have told them no – that I was busy. It is getting to be a little much for me."

"You look exhausted again. When was the last time that you had a good night's sleep?"

"I think it was some time in the late 70's."

"Good one. What can I get you something to drink?"

"Just a Pepsi, if you have one?"

"I do. Go sit down and relax, I will bring it to you."

Bill went into the living room and sat in the lounge chair and took a deep relaxing breath.

Rose came in with a glass of Pepsi.

"Do you want the TV on?"

"Sure." Bill replied.

"What's on?" Rose wondered out loud.

"The golf should be on – NBC or channel 5."

"There you go. I have made homemade beef soup if that is, OK? I just have to make the noodles."

"That is perfect."

"Ok – should be ready in about 20 minutes."

"Sounds good." Replied Bill.

Rose retreated to the kitchen and started heating the soup and cooking the noodles. Things were ready and the table set in about 20 minutes as Rose predicted.

She went into the living room to let Bill know that the soup was ready and found him sound asleep. Actually, in a very deep sleep – out cold. She turned the sound down on the TV, put a blanket over Bill and checked the time. It was 3 PM. She thought, he needs the sleep more than the food. I will give him an hour and wake him at 4. She turned down the heat on the soup and set the noodles aside.

Rose checked on Bill at 4 but there was no change, still out. She went and got her Bosch book and sat in the chair next to Bill and started reading. She got into the book and next time she looked up it was 6 PM. She needed a break from reading so she headed into her bedroom to watch TV without disturbing Bill. She started to wonder how long this would go on. Bill had been saying that he didn't sleep much – he is making up for that now. After watching some King of Queens re-runs it was now 8 PM. She went back to check on Bill.

Still no change. This is nuts she began thinking. Now not sure what to do – she hated to wake him as he obviously needed to sleep. She decided to put the soup away so it didn't spoil and clean up the kitchen. It was now 9 PM and he is still out.

Rose was still in her church clothes from this morning. So, she decided to get changed, washed up and into her PJ's and robe. After all of that and little more TV it was now 10 PM and after checking on Bill saw that he was still fast asleep. She began wondering if he is OK.

She decided to lay on the couch in the living room and wait for him to wake up. Rose was out about 5 minutes after her head hit the couch. The next thing she knows, she is opening her eyes to check on Bill and he is awake looking her.

Rose was a little embarrassed and sat up quickly. "Sorry about that – what time is it?"

"I think it is around midnight. How long have I been asleep?"

"About 9 hours! How long have you been awake?"

"Only about 10 minutes – I didn't want to wake you. Nine hours, that's insane. I haven't slept that long since high school."

"Hey – you were tired, you've been killing yourself. Rose noticed that his face looked refreshed."

"Oh my God, I ruined another dinner. What the hell is going on with me?"

"No big deal, the soup is back in the fridge. We can have it another time."

"Do you mind if I use the restroom?"

"No – follow me."

Rose led him to the full bath in her bedroom vs the half bath off of the living room.

"Use this one. I put some towels out for you and a robe if you want to take a quick shower or refreshen up."

"Rose, I need to get out of your hair. I have now ruined your entire weekend."

"We still have to eat something, you must hungry. I will make something quick while you freshen up."

Bill agreed and headed into the bathroom while Rose headed back into the kitchen. She decided on pancakes as she knew that she could whip those up quickly. She heard the shower running and knew that Bill was showering and not just washing up. That gave her a few extra minutes. It also made her wonder where this evening or night was heading.

When Bill emerged, he was wearing the robe that Rose had given him.

"A snug fit." Bill stated and Rose noticed that the robe was a little tight around the middle.

"It was my son's robe from a few years ago and looks good on you. A little small but good. Are you OK with pancakes?"

"Absolutely, that sounds perfect."

Rose served the pancakes and Bill devoured them. They talked about what a crazy weekend it had been. Rose asked about his time at the hospital on Friday, Saturday and Sunday.

"Why did they call you and who called you?"

"Erin in the CC." Bill answered. "A young boy was in for treatment from Mooseheart. Mooseheart is an orphanage a few miles from the hospital. The orphanage had dropped the child off but didn't have anyone to stay with him. He was very scared. Erin said that he was trembling and she was afraid that he was having a breakdown. I was able to calm him down but the doctor decided to keep him overnight because his blood work was not good. One thing led to another, so I stayed with him until they released him this morning."

Rose felt that Bill was finally opening up to her and willing to talk to her about what he did.

Bill was helping Rose clear the table and put things away and load the dishwasher. She could sense that he was standing next to her and looking at her. She turned toward him and Bill put his hand on her arm.

"Rose it has been a while since I have had – ah – you know feelings, romantic feelings for a woman. I really like you and" – before Bill could finish the sentence Rose leaned in and planted a passionate kiss on Bill's lips – which he returned in kind. They separated briefly, Bill smiled and then passionately embraced Rose with a bear hug to go along with another kiss.

When they separated this time, Bill mentioned that he hadn't done this in a while.

Rose responded. "You remember what goes where – right?"

"Yes, I do." Bill replied. With that, Rose took his hand and led him into the bedroom. Leaving the rest of the kitchen clean-up for tomorrow.

When they got into the bedroom, Rose stopped and turned to Bill. "You know, I have never done this with a white man."

"Well, that makes two of us." Bill replied.

8 – A NEW DAY

It was a great night for both Bill and Rose. After making love they relaxed and talked and slept a little. As the sun started to break through the window, Rose was awakened by Bill snuggling up next to her and she could tell immediately that he was ready for round 2. When they finished the sun was now fully up and lighting up the bedroom.

"Crap, what time is it?" Rose asked. She rolled over and looked at the Alexa on the night stand and the digital display showed 8:18 AM. "Crap, I am to be going to be late."

"Rose – how long have you been at Delnor?"

"I don't know, five or six weeks – why?"

"You get one sick day or personal day for every month. Take one today."

"I hate to do that. They will have to scramble to find someone to cover for me."

"No, that is part of Katie's job, so not a big deal."

"I am not even sure about who to call and what to say."

"You just ask for Janet Davies and her assistant will answer and you say that you need to take a personal day today. Then we can relax and go out to lunch."

That all sounded good to Rose but she wasn't sure.

"Bill – what about you? You haven't missed a day at Delnor in years. They may send out the police if you don't show up."

"I know but it's time. I am definitely not going in today."

"OK – if you're not, I am not. Where is my phone?"

Rose picked up her phone off of the night stand and did just as Bill had suggested. Janet's assistant did not answer, so Rose left a voice mail. She then called again and left a message for Belynda at the reception desk. Now her conscious was clear.

Rose then laid back down next to Bill who hadn't moved through all the morning commotion. Both were still naked under the covers and just enjoying being a little naughty for the first time in quite a while.

After about five minutes, Rose heard the front door to her apartment open.

Stephanie came into Rose's apartment as planned and as she had done a hundred times before. However, she noticed immediately that there was a pile of dishes in the sink and the dishwasher was left open. Something wasn't right.

"Mama, are you home?"

"Crap." Rose exclaimed as she jumped out of bed. She hurried over to close the bedroom door. Then started scrambling to find her PJ's and robe which were all over the place due to how they were taken off last night. Bill was going through the same process but in a much calmer and less frantic manner and he only had a robe to put on.

"What am I going to tell my daughter? She can't see us like this."

"Why not? We shouldn't be ashamed. The truth is always best."

"Yes, but sometimes shocking and more difficult to explain." Rose replied.

Stephanie called out again, a little louder this time. "Mama, are you home?" Stephanie was now in the hallway about halfway to the bedroom door.

"Yes hon, I will be out in a minute."

Rose could hear her walking back to the kitchen.

"She is your daughter Rose. I will go along with whatever you want me to do. I can hide in the shower until she leaves."

"Don't be ridiculous." Rose paused for a couple of minutes thinking over the options. "Come with me." She took Bill by the hand and starting heading back to the kitchen. As they turned the corner Stephanie was sitting at the computer desk with her back to them getting ready to print something.

"Stephanie, I want you to meet Bill. Bill Campbell."

With that Stephanie stood up and spun around. Her mouth open – she was speechless.

"Stephanie?"

"Oh – sorry – good to meet you Bill – sorry – I am a little in shock or surprised. Mama – what the hell? Why aren't you at work?"

Bill jumped in. "Good to meet you as well, Stephanie."

"Steph – I took a sick day today. Bill stopped by last night and spent the night."

"Obviously – nice robe. Is that Robert's robe?" She asked.

Rose replied. "Honey, finish your printing and I will call you later and we can talk. Unless, you want to stay for breakfast?"

"No – ah – No – I will finish and talk to you later."

"Ok – sounds good."

Stephanie printed several pages and then cut short her project and packed her things up. She decided that she would finish her project at the library so she could get out of there ASAP.

"I will talk to you later Mama. Bill it was good to meet you."

"Stephanie, it was good to meet you as well. I look forward to seeing you again."

The last part – the seeing you again part – seemed to catch Stephanie off guard. She hesitated slightly after hearing that - before leaving and closing the door.

"Well - that was fun." Bill mentioned trying to lighten things up a little.

"OMG – that is going to be an interesting conversation with her later today."

"Rose – why don't you take a shower and I will finish cleaning the kitchen. We can then go get some lunch or breakfast."

"OK but I need some coffee. Do you want a cup?"

"No – I never drink coffee. I have never had coffee or tea. One of the many strange things about me."

"Yes – that is a little different but I have a few strange habits of my own."

Off Rose went into her bedroom to shower and change. About 30 minutes later she returned to the kitchen. Bill had washed and dried all of the dishes and put them away. The kitchen was spotless, back to the way Rose normally kept it.

Bill noticed Rose when she returned. "Wow – you look nice."

"Thanks, so does the kitchen. Everything in the dishwasher?"

"No – I just washed them the old-fashioned way and put them away – if that is OK."

"OK, with me. Do you use the dishwasher at home?"

"No never, seems like a waste just for me. When I am finished eating, I just wash what I have used and put them away - another strange habit."

"Not so strange, probably makes sense."

"Bill, do you want to take a shower and get dressed now."

"No, I need a change of clothes. Why don't I drive us to my house. I will then take a quick shower and change and we can go to lunch."

OK – sounds like a plan – Rose, replied.

Bill went to Rose's bedroom, got dressed and was back ready to go in 5 minutes.

Out they went and down the elevator to Bill's car. As they were heading for the parking lot, Rose was wondering which car was his. As if Bill could read her mind – "it's the gray Ford Explorer."

Bill opened the door and let Rose in. The car was very clean outside and inside. "You keep a clean car." Rose noted. "Thanks." Bill replied.

They pulled out of the apartment complex and headed back down Randall Rd., south toward the hospital.

Rose asked. "So where do you live?"

"I live In the Red Gate Acres subdivision and have been there about 25 years. There it is on the left." Bill pointed out his driver side window.

He made a left turn into the subdivision and then followed the curving road to a long cul-de-sac. Rose was looking at the houses as he was driving. They were all larger homes than she was used to. All were 4 to 5,000 square feet, most were constructed of brick and all were on lots that were well over an acre.

"Nice neighborhood." Rose mentioned.

"We built this house. This was farmland back 25 years ago – just being developed." Bill took a right turn and pulled into a driveway. "This is it."

"Nice house."

As Bill pulled the car into the garage, a little panic attack swept over Rose. All of a sudden, she didn't feel like she belonged here. She was thinking this is not my house, this is not my kind of house or my kind of neighborhood. I don't belong here. The thought that this was Bill's deceased wife's house also flashed across Rose's mind.

Bill put the car into park and stepped out but Rose didn't move. He got his bag out of the back seat and noticed that Rose hadn't moved.

He leaned into the still open driver's side door. "Rose, it's OK, you can come in."

"Maybe I will wait for you here"

"Rose, I went into your home."

"Not the same thing."

With that Bill closed the driver's side door. Rose not sure what was going to happen. Bill walked around the back of the car and opened the passenger side where Rose was sitting. He put his hand out to Rose. "Rose, it's OK." With that, Rose put her hand into Bill's and he held it all the way into the house.

When they got inside, Bill continued to hold Rose's hand as he gave her a quick tour of the house. The house did not look lived in. There was no clutter and everything was neat, clean and organized. "Looks like a model home." Rose mentioned.

"Obviously, much larger than I need."

Bill showed her around the first floor and into his office. One wall was all book shelves. Here was the clutter. In addition to what looked like a thousand books were photos, nick knacks, awards and one large framed Hole-in-One certificate.

Rose asked. "Have you read all of these books?"

"Yes. I use to travel a lot on business and read a lot on the plane."

Rose walked past the book shelves seeing business books, a lot of history and biography books and some fiction books as well. "I don't see any Michael Connelly books?"

"Those are upstairs." Bill replied.

"You got a hole-in-one?" Rose asked while looking at the certificate.

"Yes, a few years ago."

Rose also got a good view of Bill's family and wife as there had to be 20 pictures in a variety of frames across the book shelves. There was also a fair number of scenery photos from travels around the world.

Bill seemed anxious to move along as he stood by the door. He asked if Rose wanted to see the upstairs?

"Sure." Rose replied.

There were four spacious bedrooms upstairs and two full bathrooms. Bill didn't go into any but Rose noticed another desk and more book shelves and wandered into that room. "What is this – another office?"

"Yes – it was originally my son's bedroom. Recently, I made it my 2nd or upstairs office. There are the Michael Connelly books."

The Michael Connelly books were all in a row in the bottom shelf of a bedside table. Bill's desk in this room had large book shelves across the top that were also full of books. More books, Rose noted.

"Well, that is the tour." Bill stated as he led Rose back downstairs. He went through the kitchen and family room and opened what looked like patio doors. They entered into a screened-in porch. The porch had a great view of the backyard and a large flat screen TV on one wall, a large table and chairs and love seat as well as bar or cooler place for drinks.

"Bill, this is a great room or porch."

"Yes – my favorite room and where I spend most of my time."

"I can see why."

"Why don't you wait here while I change. Do you want something to drink?"

"No, I am good."

Bill turned on the TV and handed the controller to Rose. "Put on whatever you want."

Rose turned off the TV and sat in one of the swivel chairs that surrounded the table. She leaned back to take in the view and collect her thoughts. She needed to discuss some things with Bill before this went any further.

Bill returned in about 15 minutes looking refreshed, showered, shaved and changed into new clothes. He asked Rose how she was doing and whether she wanted to go get some lunch.

"Bill, we need to talk a little before we go."

"OK – hold on." Bill replied. Off he went into the kitchen. When he returned, he had two glasses of Pepsi. One he put in front of Rose and the other he put in front of the chair next to Rose. "OK – let's talk." Sitting in the chair next to Rose.

Rose started slowly not sure exactly where to begin. "First, I haven't been completely honest with you."

"In what way." Bill asked.

"That meeting with Janet was more than just about what happened on the 5th floor. It was also about you. She was like warning me about getting involved with you. Wait – that doesn't sound right. She said that there would be nothing wrong with us dating. However, she was just cautioning me about getting involved with you. Her concern is that because you are so well thought of at the hospital that people are protective and concerned about you. As such, that people would notice and people would talk."

Bill didn't respond – just sat there thinking.

So, Rose continued. "Bill, Janet was not the first person who warned me about the same thing. I was told that many other ladies had attempted to connect with you and you rejected them. Also, that you didn't show for many events to which you were invited."

Rose paused again to see if Bill wanted to respond. "Go ahead." He stated.

"Bill why did you ask me to lunch that first day that we met? That and the other lunches were way out of character for you." Rose paused and said – "say something."

"Rose, I have no idea why I asked you to lunch that first day. It just happened. It was an instinctive reaction to meeting you. I can't explain it – maybe just an instant connection. Whatever it was, I felt something and reacted to it. If it had been a mistake and not gone well, it would have been over in 10 minutes. But it wasn't, it was just the opposite. The feeling I had toward you just deepened every time that I was with you and when I wasn't with you, you were always on my mind. I haven't had that feeling in over 50 years - when I met my wife."

"As far as that other stuff about me rejecting people, I just wasn't ready or interested in connecting with anyone after my wife passed. I was talked out – just kind of empty inside. The only people that I talked to were my sons."

"We had a lot friends, neighbors and cousins. But they were all couple friends and it just didn't feel right being with them without my wife. I have lost connection with all of them. I wondered if I would ever meet anyone again who caught my attention and had about given up – until that day that I met you."

Bill paused, looking at Rose. "Good answer." Rose stated.

"What else." Bill asked?

"Well Bill, we live in and come from different worlds – black/white, rich/poor, conservative/liberal. You know that I really like you, at least I hope that you do. I don't want to head down a road where it is destined to end badly and both of us get hurt."

"Rose – don't fall into the trap of putting labels on people and letting that determine what you think of them. I have been lucky enough to travel around the world and have worked with people in Asia, Europe, North America and South America. What I have learned is that people are people everywhere. Where they are from, how they look, what their job is, how much money they have or who they vote for – doesn't define them as people."

"Also, I am too old to worry about tomorrow or next week or next year. I know how I feel about you right now and I want to pursue that as long and passionately as possible. When problems occur, and they will – we will face them head on – together.

Bill then continued. "Yes, I am a conservative – yes, I am financially well off – yes, I am white – and yes – even though you didn't ask, I voted for Donald Trump and I would do so again."

Bill paused to see if Rose was going to say something. When she didn't – Bill added – "Rose, it is really up to you. I know you are a good person and I really like you. I am ready to continue our relationship and see where it goes. The question is – are we getting lunch or am I driving you home? So, what do you say?"

Without hesitation Rose stood up and asked – "where are we going for lunch?"

9 – FAMILY

Three Months Later –

Things have settled down for Rose – and Bill. Their relationship was now public knowledge at Delnor and generally accepted by everyone. Rose still felt a little tension from the nurses up on 5, but nothing that she couldn't handle. Rose and Bill sat down with Janet to make sure there was no issue that would impact Rose's job and Janet confirmed that there was no problem. Bill was no longer volunteering every day. He was now coming in 3 or 4 days a week and almost never on weekends. The overnight or extended stays by Bill were still happening, but they are much rarer and limited to really severe cases. Whenever Bill was at Delnor, lunch was still part of the regular routine for Bill & Rose.

On the personal side, the relationship continued to blossom without any major hiccups. Bill and Rose were still in "the falling in love" part of their relationship, which is always the best part. Everything they did together was new and held some excitement in spite of their age. Even places they had been before or experiences that they had before as individuals seemed new and exciting again as they experienced them together for the first time.

The sex aspect continued to be great for both of them. They spent most weekends together and that often developed into 4 or 5 days depending on what was going on. They had taken several trips. One was to Palm Springs so Bill could golf. One to NYC because Rose had never been there. Also, to San Francisco so they could visit Yosemite – which neither had been to before. Initially, most of the overnight stays were at Rose's apartment as she was not completely comfortable at Bill's home. Likely having something to do with that being the home that he shared with his wife. However, now his place became the more frequent weekend place as it just gave them more room and the screened porch was just so comfortable.

The challenging part of the relationship, as you might expect was dealing with family and friends. Bill didn't have many friends. All of his friends had been couples that he and his wife hung with or were relatives (cousins) of his wife. Once his wife passed all of those relationships passed away as well. Initially, they invited Bill to all of their social events, but he had no interest in going alone as it only served to remind him what he was missing. He had his golf guys which he was now seeing more frequently. He had started playing again but he didn't socialize with them outside of golf. Although Bill belonged to the local country club, he just used it for golf. He nor his wife ever socialized there, except for occasionally using the restaurant for dinner and even that was very rare.

So, that brings us to family!

BILL'S SIDE –

Bill called both of his sons to tell them that he was dating. Both were surprised but not shocked. Bill had not said anything about Rose to them before calling them. Both boys got quiet when Bill told them about dating. Bill just assumed that both thought that he was too old to date and would just live out the rest of his life alone. Both were also a little surprised that the woman's name was Rose, the same as their mother. Both were also surprised when he told them that she was black.

Bill realized that it was a lot to take in on one phone call. As such, he didn't press them for a reaction or feedback to the info that he had just dropped on them. He let them absorb it and then moved the conversation to other topics. He ended the call with both by saying that he wanted them to meet Rose as soon as possible. Neither boy jumped at the suggestion so Bill didn't press them.

In an effort to have his boys meet Rose in a less formal setting, Bill suggested a Saturday lunch to Rose. The lunch would be at the club, after golfing with the boys. Although Rose was anxious to meet them, she was scared to death! Normally, the race thing would have been the big issue but Rose knew that the bigger issue was another woman with the same name as their mother being with their father. That was going to be just weird for the boys.

The plan was not to tell the boys about the lunch with Rose in advance but rather to mention it during the round. The three of them would always stop for lunch in the club after a round of golf. Today, Rose would simply meet them in the restaurant. During the round he told them that Rose may meet them for lunch. Bill wanted it to seem like it wasn't a sure thing. Just to gage their reaction. Neither boy reacted negatively to the news so he texted Rose on the 17th tee to come to the club.

Rose was off the charts nervous waiting for the three golfers in the restaurant. First, she had only been to the club twice and each time she was the only black person in the building. Even the bartenders and waiters were all white. Also, she had previously always been with Bill when going into the club and now she was entering alone. She was thinking that they might not let her in. She had no problem getting seated in the restaurant as Bill had told her just to mention his name. However, sitting there alone, seemed to last forever.

During the round, Bill took advantage of having the two boys together. He questioned them about their feelings and reaction to the call that he had made to them when he told them about Rose.

Matthew being the oldest spoke first. "Dad, I am fine with it. It is going to take a little time to get use to the situation. You can't expect things to be the same as they were with Mom."

Bill responded. "Matthew, I agree and understand that things will obviously not be the same as before. Nobody is trying to replace your mother. I am simply dating someone whom I like a lot. I want to be able to have her around when we get together without it seeming weird or causing the two of you or her to be uncomfortable. I know that this whole situation is made stranger because her name is the same as your mother's. My new friend Rose, isn't your mother. I know that and she knows that."

"Dad, I am OK with that but we will see how things go. If she is a good person and everyone gets along, it should not be a problem."

Bill then turned to David and asked – "well?"

"What do you want me to say? It is very weird Dad, that you have a girlfriend at your age. Losing Mom was hard enough and now you are adding a stranger to the mix. I have no idea how that is going to work. Let's play golf."

Bill decided not to respond to him and let things settle down and see if David stays for lunch.

After the round, Bill and his sons walked into the grill room for lunch. Rose was waiting and stood up when Bill approached. Bill could tell that Rose was nervous so he walked up and took her hand and gave her a kiss before introducing her to the boys. The kiss helped Rose settle down. He introduced both David and Matthew before sitting down.

The group ordered drinks and the guys made a lot of small talk about their round of golf and their scores, while Rose just listened. When the conversation paused, Rose spoke up. "Matthew – David – I know that this is really weird for you and I want to thank you for having lunch with me. I just want you to know that I really like your dad and my hope is that over time we can become good friends and family."

Bill reached over touched her hand when she finished – saying "thanks."

Neither Matthew nor David responded immediately. After an awkward pause, Matthew finally spoke up saying, "we hope so as well Rose".

The rest of the lunch went well. Bill and Rose both tried to guide the conversation and create opportunity for the boys to have direct discussion with Rose. When lunch ended, both boys shook hands with Rose and said goodbye.

Overall, the lunch seemed to go well. Over the next few months, Bill worked at getting them together with Matthew and David. They had some luck with Matthew as they had a couple of dinners with Matthew and his wife Maggie. Matthew also came over to Bill's house a couple of times on his own to help his dad with computer issues. Matthew also brought his dog Pete. Pete and Rose became good friends as Rose was good at giving Pete treats. David was a bigger challenge. They were only able to get one lunch with David. He was fine during the lunch but just reluctant to get together. Bill figured just too painful for David as he still missed his mother.

Rose never felt that her race was an issue for the boys. This was a concern going in, but the boys seemed to have the same attitude as Bill – people are people. She could definitely tell that both boys were republicans, conservatives and very well informed about social, political and economic issues.

Bill and Rose both felt that they had made progress with the boys but that there was still a lot of room for improvement in the relationship.

ROSE'S SIDE –

Bill and Rose were having frequent interactions with her children and with her friends. Most had been fine, but she could also feel the relationship with her friends changing. She didn't see them near as often as she did before Bill and certainly talked to them less frequently. Even her relationship with her best friend GG, seemed to have changed. When she first met Bill and they would go to dinner or to the movies, everything seemed fine. However, over time, it was clear that the dynamic between Rose and GG was not the same.

The relationship between Stephanie and Bill seemed to be the best among her family and friends. Stephanie would talk business about the Hallmark store that she managed. Bill has a lot of business experience and is very good at giving advice to Stephanie when needed. He even spent a lot of time helping her with the stores accounting system. It was heartwarming for Rose to see them get into deep and long discussions about the store.

Stephanie's son Jordan was the big concern for the family. He had always struggled in school and he didn't seem to be improving. He didn't have any friends and was hooked on video games. Next year he would be heading into high school and Stephanie was worried about how he would adapt. She also had concerns about him ever going to college. The good news was that Jordan seemed to like Bill and seemed to have a connection with him. Bill seemed to be able to draw Jordan out a little and get him to engage in discussions which was rare for Jordan.

Jordan was currently the big issue for Stephanie and Rose. He was on summer break and there was nothing to distract Jordan away from the video games during the day. He was too young to get a job and too old for a baby sitter. Stephanie and her husband tried to sign him up for soccer and baseball summer camps like the other kids, but Jordan wasn't interested. He seemed to have the talent, but didn't like the social interaction and pressure. Jordan seemed to like being alone with his computer and video games and that really bothered Rose and his parents.

Stephanie's daughter, Kelly – was the opposite of her brother. She was a good student and very social and outgoing. She had a large number of friends – both boys and girls. Although only in 5th grade, she was very attractive like her grandmother. The boys seem to be buzzing around her already. Although she wasn't hooked on video games like her brother, she was hooked on her cell phone. She was on it constantly mostly texting. She was taking two summer school classes. The classes were not because of bad grades, as she was an honor roll student. She was taking the classes simply to get ahead and spend time with friends.

Rose's son Robert on the other hand only tolerated Bill for his mother's sake. He was a super lib, watching MSNBC every night. He hated that his mom was dating a white man and hated even more that he was a one percenter, a conservative and likely a Trump supporter. That made him a bad guy no matter what his mother said about all the good things that he did. He also hated that Stephanie had crossed over and appeared to not only accept Bill, but was moving down the same capitalistic path that Bill had done. Bill was smart enough to pick up on Robert's feelings. He walked on egg shells whenever he was around him, so that he wouldn't say the wrong thing and set off Robert.

Rose had wanted Bill to attend Sunday church with her each week, but he declined. Rose thought that it would be a means of introducing Bill to more of her friends but Bill wasn't interested. It wasn't that Bill wasn't religious, just the opposite – he and his wife attended their catholic church every Sunday. Attending church without his wife simply brought back too many memories. Also, Bill played golf on Sunday mornings – that was his excuse anyway. Rose would normally meet Bill at his house after church for lunch. He would be getting back from golf about the same time as Rose got there after church.

THIS PARTICULAR SUNDAY ROSE and Bill were having a late lunch on the porch at Bill's home. Bill had made filet sliders, his favorite – on the grill. They were watching the Cubs and the Brewers play at Wrigley while eating lunch.

"Rose, have you been to Milwaukee to see a Cubs/Brewers game at Miller Park?"

"No, I have not."

"OK - I will get us tickets. It is a great place to watch a game and only about 90 minutes away."

"Bill, we haven't even been to a game at Wrigley yet. You said that we were going to go to a Cubs game but we haven't."

"You are right. I will get us Cub tickets Wrigley first, but I will also get us tickets for Miller Park as well."

"Do you think that Jordan would like going to a Cubs game? Even if he doesn't like baseball, hot dogs, popcorn, ice cream and Pepsi – that could hook him."

"Why not? It is worth a shot. Thanks for thinking about him."

"Rose's phone buzzed, it was a call from Stephanie – Hey Mama, how are you doing – what are you doing?"

"Just having lunch with Bill."

"Where at?"

"His place, on the porch watching the Cubs game."

"Nice. Hey, what is your schedule this week at the hospital?"

"Working every day – 9 to 5 as usual. Why?"

"I have a problem. Eddie is traveling this week for work. I have inventory at the store Monday thru Wednesday and the Regional Manager is coming in on Wednesday, which means dinner with her. I don't want to leave my kids alone all day and into the night. Kelly can stay with her friend Sam but Jordan will be all alone. Just wondering if you have any suggestions?"

"Bill was listening to Rose's side of the conversation and could figure out what the issue was. Rose, he interrupted her conversation – I can watch Jordan. I have nothing going on."

"Steph, hold on – as Rose put her hand over the phone. Bill, I can't ask you to do that."

"You are not asking me – I am suggesting it. I don't mind. It will be good for me to connect with Jordan. Rose simply replied – OK."

"Stephanie – Bill is willing to take Jordan. There was a pause as Stephanie considered this option and knew she was desperate. OK, she replied."

"What time tomorrow morning?" Rose asked Stephanie.

"7 AM, if that is not too early."

Rose turned to Bill. Is 7AM OK for picking up Jordan?

"No problem, I will be there."

With that Rose and Stephanie made some small talk and Rose finished by saying – "OK Steph, I have to get back to my lunch."

"Bye Mama." She then hung up.

Bill and Rose finished their lunch and finished watching the Cubs. They won 5 to 4.

Rose told Bill that she needed to go home tonight as she had been at Bill's since Thursday of last week. She had to do some laundry and get ready for work tomorrow. Staying at Bill's was great, but it through off her schedule of food shopping the dry cleaning. She now had to fit those in during the week after work. Both were on her mind for tomorrow night.

"Rose, a couple of things about tomorrow. First, I have no idea where Stephanie lives."

"OK – I will text you with her address."

"Also, what time should I bring him home?"

"Good question – we didn't talk about that. She has inventory so she might be working late. Just bring him by my place and I will make us dinner. Make it around 6 PM as I have to stop by the Jewel and drop off some cleaning on the way home."

"OK sounds like a plan. He gave Rose a kiss and she got into her car and headed home."

10 – FORE

Bill had raised two boys so he didn't have much concern about spending a couple days with Jordan. The worst-case scenario was that he was not able to connect with him and Jordan spent most of the time playing video games, which he would have done if he was home anyway.

Stephanie and Eddie lived in a townhouse in a newer neighborhood not that far from Rose's apartment. It was a three bedroom, 2 1/2 bath unit with a finished basement. They had purchased the unit about 3 years ago and were very happy with the townhouse.

Bill showed up at Stephanie's front door at 7 AM sharp as requested. He had a game plan for the day but was prepared to change it, if things didn't go as planned. Stephanie opened the door and invited Bill inside. Her place was not as neat and organized as Rose's - which was not surprising. Jordan was there waiting with his arms full of video game equipment. He had his handheld device in one hand and a tablet in the other. Stephanie then gave Bill Jordan's lunch box and a bag of snacks.

"Stephanie – you didn't need to give me all this food. I was just going to take Jordan somewhere to eat or get fast food."

"Oh – he is pretty fussy about what he will eat. Thought it would be easier just to give you his normal stuff. You have my cell number if you need me - right?"

"No - I don't but I can get it from Rose if I need it. I plan to bring him back to Rose's about 6 and you can pick him up there. Is that OK?"

"Yes. I really appreciate this, Bill. What do you have planned for today?"

"Nothing special, just going to hang out. I am looking forward to it."

"Ready Jordan? "Let's rock" - Bill said to him. With that they were out the door and heading for Bill's car.

Instead of heading for his house, Bill decided to go to the country club. It was a beautiful sunny summer day and he hated the thought of being inside. There was not much conversation between Bill and Jordan as he was seated in the backseat at Stephanie's direction. When they got to the country club and Bill exited the car, Jordan looked a little confused and worried about where they were. Bill jumped out of the car and told Jordan to leave his video games in the car and follow him.

They went into the pro-shop where Bill introduced Jordan to the head and assistant pros. "Jordan needs a set of clubs." Bill mentioned to the head pro.

Brian, the head Pro replied. "No problem, follow me." Bill and Jordan followed Brian out to where the carts were parked and asked one of the attendants to get a set of rental clubs. The attendant had already put Bill's clubs on the cart and then he loaded the rental clubs. Bill asked Brian if the course was crowded. Brian responded. "No, it should be wide open for you."

"OK, let's go Jordan." Bill stated. Bill got into the cart, but he sat in the passenger seat. Jordan was confused and hesitated looking at Bill. "Jordan, you are driving buddy!" Jordan stepped into the cart with hesitation not having driven a cart or anything else before. Bill pointed down the path to the first tee – "head that way." Jordan put both hands on the wheel and stepped on the gas. There was a little jerk to the cart as Jordan got use to the pedal, but then things settled down quickly. "You're a natural." Bill stated. Bill could read Jordan's face – he saw real excitement for the first time.

When they got to the first tee, Bill then started to explain and show Jordan how the golf thing worked. Bill put a tee in the ground and placed a ball on it and after a couple of practice swings, hit a drive. Jordan was standing behind Bill watching the process. Jordan went to get a club, but Bill said – "not yet Jordan." "Let's go find the ball first." They then jumped back into the cart and drove down the first fairway to Bill's ball. Jordan was still getting the hang of driving. The tee was elevated so the drive down the fairway had some speed and excitement to it which wasn't lost on Jordan. When they got to Bill's ball, he selected a club – a 7 iron – and Bill hit his ball up to just short of the green. Bill was talking continuously during the entire process, explaining everything to Jordan. He was getting no feedback from Jordan, but Bill thought that he was listening. Bill then chipped and putted his ball into the hole, continuing to explain everything to Jordan along the way.

They then got back into the cart and drove to the second tee. Bill asked Jordan if he wanted to hit a ball. Jordan responded with an emphatic – "yes!"

Bill showed him how to get a tee and ball from his bag. He then taught him how to put the tee in the ground and how high to tee up the ball. He explained to Jordan which clubs were for driving and allowed Jordan to select his driver from the bag. Bill then showed him the swing basics and where to stand. He had him make several practice swings and made some corrections to his grip and arms. "OK, Jordan, hit away." Bill said and stood back to watch.

His first swing ever was pretty amazing. He didn't hit it very far – maybe 150 yards, but it was solid contact and it was straight. With that swing, Jordan was hooked. The change to his demeanor, expressions, and talkativeness were immediate. Bill hit his drive and off they went. Bill continued to coach Jordan on every shot and every aspect of the game. Jordan hit some good shots and some bad shots, but never lost interest or got discouraged. Which is not common for many beginner golfers.

At the half-way house after the 9th hole, Bill asked Jordan if he wanted to stop and head back home. Jordan responded quickly, "no let's keep playing." Bill got them each a Pepsi and off they went to the 10th hole. To Bill's amazement they played all 18 holes. Bill wasn't keeping score for Jordan or himself, but rather just coaching Jordan and watching for signs of fatigue which he did not see. The other thing that Bill noticed was that Jordan was listening and learning. He seldom had to tell him the same think twice and was steadily improving throughout the round.

Bill had heard about Jordan struggling in school and Bill immediately knew that his struggles were not because of a lack of intelligence, but rather a lack of interest.

When they got to the clubhouse it was about 11:30 – meaning that they had been playing about 4 hours. That is amazing for Jordan's first time. They went inside to the grill room. Bill ordered a hamburger and asked Jordan what he wanted. Hot dog please, he responded. Jordan was a different person over lunch. Bill engaged him over a variety of topics from golf to school stuff to TV shows and Jordan was responsive and engaging like he had never seen him before.

When lunch was over, Jordan asked if they could play some more. Bill said no but they could practice their chipping and putting – to which Jordan enthusiastically replied great! They spent the next couple of hours putting, chipping, and hitting out of sand traps. It was now 2:30 and Bill knew that was enough for his first day of golf. So, they headed to Bill's house for a little R & R. Bill intentionally left the video games in the car when they went inside. Jordan was a little amazed at the size of the house. Bill put the Cubs game on the TV and sat down in his favorite chair. Jordan took a seat next to him on the couch. After about 5 minutes Bill looked over and Jordan was out – nap time. Bill put his head back and after about 5 minutes he was out as well.

It was about 3:30 when Bill woke up. He looked over and Jordan was still out. The Cubs were still playing, but losing 7 to 1. Jordan woke up at about 4. The Cubs were making a furious comeback, but lost in extra innings 8 to 7. Jordan appeared to watch the extra innings with interest or maybe was doing so because Bill was so interested. It was hard to know for sure.

Bill asked Jordan if he knew who Tiger Woods was. "Of course." Jordan replied. Bill then asked if Jordan has watched him play. "No - not really." Jordan responded. Bill then asked Jordan to follow him and headed into his office.

Bill showed Jordan his hole-in-one plaque that he had received from the country club. He then sat Jordan down at the computer. "Jordan, google Tiger Woods swing." Bill instructed. Jordan, did as instructed. Immediately up came an endless list of You Tube videos showing Tiger Woods swinging a golf club. Some were instructional videos, some were showing his best shots, and others were simply golf commentators analyzing his swing. Bill told him to take a look at some of those videos.

Bill left the room telling Jordan that he would be right back. He went into the kitchen and got a glass of water and sat down at the counter. He sat there for about 10 minutes and then headed back into his office to check on Jordan.

"So, what do you think?" Bill asked.

"He is amazing. Can we go see him play?"

"Yes, but Tiger was been injured and isn't playing right now. He will be playing again soon and when he does, we will go see him."

"Have you seen him play?"

"Yes, several times when he was playing in the Chicago area."

"Wow. Can I keep looking at more videos?"

"Sure, I will come get you when it is time to leave."

He picked up the latest Michael Connelly book that he was reading as he left his office. He sat down at the kitchen counter again and started reading. He had gotten through several chapters when his phone buzzed. It was a text from Rose. "Where are you guys?"

Bill responded. "We are on our way. Be there in 15."

"Jordan, we have to go." Bill yelled. He heard no movement from Jordan so he walked down the hallway to the office door. "Jordan, let's go, we are late." They jumped in the car and off they went.

They arrived at Rose's about 15 minutes later and about 30 minutes later than Rose was expecting. Rose was waiting for them at the front door to the building. She welcomed both and gave her grandson a hug asking him if he was hungry?

Yes, I am starving Grandma?

When they got up to Rose's apartment, she instructed Jordan to go wash his hands before eating. After Jordan went to wash his hands as instructed, Rose turned to Bill and gave him a hug and kiss asked how things went today with Jordan?

"Things went great today. Sorry that we are late. We were on the computer and lost track of time."

"On the computer? Doing what?"

"Watching videos."

"What kind of videos?" Rose asked.

"Golf videos." Bill was being intentionally vague with his answers just to keep Rose guessing.

"Well, dinner is ready, let's eat." Rose stated. She figured that she would hear about the video thing later.

Just as they were sitting down for Jordan's favorite meal, which is chicken nuggets and mac-&-cheese, the door opened and Stephanie came in.

"Just in time." Rose told her. Stephanie didn't respond to Rose.

Instead, she greeted Bill asked him about his day. "How did things go with Jordan today?"

"Things went great! Couldn't have been better."

With that, Jordan came into the kitchen. "Grandma, when are we eating? I am starving!"

"Right now. Don't you say hello to your mother?"

"Hi Mom." Jordan quickly said.

So, they sat down and started to eat dinner. Immediately, Stephanie started asking Jordan what he did today.

Jordan – with a mouth full of food, started to explain but Rose interrupted. "Jordan, don't talk with your mouth full!"

"Yes, Grandma."

After swallowing and taking a drink of water, Jordan started over. "Well, we played golf. Then, we had lunch and played some more golf after lunch. Then we went to Bill's. He let me use his computer and I watched videos."

"What kind of videos?" Stephanie asked.

"Tiger Woods videos."

"Oh." Stephanie answered in a relieved tone.

Stephanie then turned to Bill. "Where did you guys play golf?"

"At the country club."

"You mean on the regular course? How is that possible? Jordan has never played golf."

"I know, but he did great. We played 18 holes and I think that he really liked it."

"Did he eat the lunch that I gave to you?"

"No, we ate at the club."

Stephanie looked a little annoyed but didn't say anything. "What about his video games?"

"Oh – they are still in my car. I will get them for you after dinner. He didn't touch them all day."

"You're kidding?"

Jordan just continued to chow down on his nuggets and Mac & Cheese, ignoring the back and forth between Bill and his mom.

"Grandma, can I have more nuggets?" Jordan asked. Rose immediately got up and put 4 more nuggets and more Mac on Jordan's plate, which he then devoured.

After dinner, Stephanie helped her mother clean up the table and put the dishes in the dishwasher. After they finished, they went into the living to check on Bill and Jordan. Bill had put on Fox News and Jordan was sitting there watching.

Stephanie was a little shocked that Fox News was on and also that Jordan was watching. Fox was the dark side and she didn't want her son exposed to it. Stephanie then said, "Jordan time to go babe."

"OK Mom." He replied.

Bill then asked Stephanie, "same time tomorrow morning – 7AM?"

"Yes." Stephanie replied with a little hesitation, but she knew that she had no other choice.

"Do you want his video games or should I just keep them since he will be with me tomorrow?"

Stephanie was just starting to reply saying, yes that Bill should go get them - when Jordan interrupted saying, "no mom, I don't need them." Stephanie was surprised by Jordan's response but then repeated to Bill, "yes – please get them."

"OK. I will get them and meet you downstairs." Bill then headed down to his car to retrieve Jordans games.

As soon as Bill left the apartment, Stephanie turned to Rose – speaking softly making sure that Jordan couldn't hear her. "Mama, Fox News – really? I don't want Jordan watching that! I am not sure Bill should watch Jordan tomorrow."

"Stephanie – it's not a big deal. Your son was outside all day and not playing video games. That's a good thing and you're worried about a little Fox News?"

Stephanie replied. "Whatever – I don't like it!" Then she yelled. "Let's go Jordan."

Bill was waiting for them when they got to parking lot. Bill handed Jordan the games and told him that he would see him in the morning. "OK great." Jordan replied. Stephanie just gave a quick wave to Bill and got into the car.

Bill headed back up to Rose's apartment. When he got inside Rose was waiting for him. She gave him a big hug and kiss. "What is that for?" Bill asked.

"Just because you are amazing and a thanks for watching Jordan today."

"Rose, he is a great kid, a pretty good golfer, and very smart in spite of his grades." Bill looked at Rose and asked if she wanted to relax and whether he should head home for the night.

"You aren't going anywhere mister." She walked over and shut the TV off. She then took Bill's hand and led him down the hallway to her bedroom.

11 – FEEDBACK

Tuesday with Jordan was a repeat of Monday. The weather was perfect and they played 18 holes in the morning and then had lunch. Like yesterday, Jordan continued to play well. He also demonstrated a good and calm demeanor throughout the day, even when he wasn't playing well.

After lunch, instead of just chipping and putting, they went to the range and Bill worked with Jordan on each of the clubs in his bag.

After hitting at the range for a couple of hours, Bill was exhausted. He and Jordan loaded their clubs back into the cart and headed back to the clubhouse. At the club house, the attendant was cleaning their clubs as Bill and Jordan waited.

Bill told Jordan to stay there a minute and went into the clubhouse to talk to the head pro. When Bill returned - he threw his golf bag over his shoulder and started heading to the car with Jordan following. Bill stopped and told Jordan – "get your bag."

Jordan looked puzzled. "But that's not mine." He stated.

"It is now." Bill replied. "It is an early birthday present from the club for playing so well."

Jordan hustled back and copying Bill, put the bag over his shoulder and followed him to the car. They put their clubs in the back of Bill's Explorer and closed the door. Jordan felt like a real golfer.

Bill then headed south on Randall Rd to Dick's Sporting goods. He purchased Jordan some golf shoes, some golf balls, a golf glove, and a couple of golf shirts and shorts. Now next time that we play, you will be ready, Bill told Jordan. Jordan seemed ecstatic and said "thank you Mr. Bill."

Bill corrected him saying – "just call me Bill."

That evening they ate dinner at Rose's just like yesterday. Today dinner was spaghetti, another one of Jordan's favorites. Stephanie grilled them with questions again and the answers were pretty much the same as yesterday. More golf and no video games, again Stephanie was amazed. She mentioned that she had finished the inventory at the store so she wouldn't need Bill tomorrow. Jordan jumped in – "Mom, I want to play golf tomorrow with Bill."

Hoping to avoid an issue between Jordan and his mother, Bill responded. "Jordan, it is supposed to rain tomorrow anyway. Let's plan to play on Thursday. You can practice chipping in the grassy area behind your house and practice putting on the carpet like I showed you.

Rose decided to change the subject. "Hey – Bill we have not talked about July 4th."

Bill asked – "what about July 4th?"

Rose and Stephanie then explained that there was an annual picnic/cookout on July 4th. It was kind of a big deal for them with about 50 family and friends, barbeque, softball, etc. Bill responded, "that sounds great. I will be there, if I am invited?"

"Yes, you are." Rose confirmed.

"Where is it at? Bill asked.

"The Elgin Woods, just off of Route 31 and I90."

"OK I have been there. It's a nice area."

It was time for everyone to head home. Bill, Stephanie and Jordan all walked out together. Rose also walked out with them to say goodbye. Bill loaded Jordan's untouched video games into the back seat of Stephanie's car. He then asked her to open her trunk because he had one more thing. He went to his car and returned with Jordan's golf bag and clubs, as well as, several shopping bags from Dick's.

"What is all this?" Stephanie asked.

"Jordan's golf stuff."

"Bill – I can't afford all of this.

"Stephanie, it is simply a gift for Jordan."

Stephanie was surprised and annoyed, but didn't want to get into it in front of Jordan.

Jordan seemed excited with all of the stuff that Bill had bought for him. "Mom, this is great stuff." Jordan stated. "I will now look like a golfer when I play." Stephanie simply rolled her eyes and got into her car. It was obvious that she was a little annoyed.

After Stephanie drove away, Bill said goodbye to Rose after asking if Stephanie would be OK. Rose told Bill that she will be fine. She said that she would call her later and make sure that she was OK.

Rose did call Stephanie later after Jordan had gone to bed. She expected that Stephanie would have settled down and that the whole golf club thing would be forgotten, but she was wrong. Stephanie didn't like that Bill had purchased Jordan golf clubs and all the other stuff. She also didn't like that Bill had been taking him to Bill's country club. Rose was shocked by her daughter's reaction.

"Stephanie, what are you talking about? Bill spent two days with Jordan. Got him outside and some needed exercise. Got him away from playing video games and watching TV all day. He exposed him to a new sport which Jordan seems to really like. He got him some golf clubs, so what? They didn't cost much. I am sorry, Stephanie – I don't see that Bill did anything wrong. In fact, I would expect that you would be thanking him."

"Mama – I don't want Jordan associating country club types. Who is he going to play golf with? None of his friends play golf. I can't afford to pay golf fees. I don't even know where to take him. Who knows how long Bill is going to be around and how long he will want to take him golfing? It is not a good idea and I wish Bill would have discussed this with me before starting down this path."

"Also, Bill spent a lot of money on Jordan the last two days. How do you think that makes me feel? He should have asked me first. We are not country club people."

"What does that mean?"

"Rich, white, conservative Trump voters, Etc. You know, Fox News watchers!"

Rose was just stunned by those words and didn't know what to say. After getting no response, Stephanie continued. "Mama, I am sorry but that is how I feel. I like Bill but I am not sure he should be hanging with Jordan."

Rose composed herself and simply replied – "OK, let's talk about this later."

Rose hung up the phone without saying goodbye. For the first time in a long time or maybe ever, she was very angry with her daughter. At the same time, she was sad and extremely frustrated. For the first time in many years, she had a man to be with that she liked a lot and who seemed to be a good person. Instead of enjoying this new chapter in her life with her daughter, she appeared to be fighting her the whole way. She couldn't imagine how her son would react?

Rose decided not to think about it. She decided to treat herself to an ice cream sundae instead. A little or lot of Hershey's Special Dark chocolate syrup is always good for easing one's frustrations.

12 – FEELINGS

Rose was at the front desk on Wednesday morning as usual. She knew she wasn't herself as the episode with Stephanie was weighing heavy on her mind. She looked up and saw Bill heading her way and that seemed to wipe her concerns away. He walked up to the reception desk and greeted with his normal good morning. That is exactly what Rose needed.

"Good morning." Rose replied.

Belynda was also behind the desk, standing about 5 feet away. "What no good morning for me, she asked?"

"Belynda – I told you not when Rose is around." Bill said with a big smile.

"You guys are hysterical." Rose stated.

Bill started heading off to the elevators. "See you at lunch?" He said to Rose as he was leaving.

"Yes. Where are you at today?" Rose asked?

"5th floor – see you later."

Rose felt much better after seeing Bill. However, as the morning wore on, the concern around her discussion with Stephanie returned. She knew that Bill was expecting to take Jordan golfing tomorrow. How would she tell him and what would she tell him about Stephanie not wanting that to happen?

She also started to think about the July 4th picnic which was now only a week away. She had invited Bill and he had accepted. Now she wasn't sure that it was a good idea for him to be there. She had Stephanie and Robert to think about. In addition, all of her other family and friends, who likely felt the same way as Stephanie and Robert. However, up to this point, they were not saying anything to her face. Since she has been seeing Bill, she rarely saw her old friends and family. She was certain that Bill was getting the blame for that.

The morning rush was over and she was just standing there thinking when Belynda spoke up. "Hey, aren't you late for lunch?"

"Crap." Rose said and she saw it was 12:05. Being late to lunch, that was a first for Rose. She rushed to the cafeteria and got her food and sat down with Bill who was waiting for her.

'Sorry, that I am late – lost track of time."

"No problem. I was a little late as well."

"What are you doing up on 5 today?"

"There is a young girl, I think about Jordan's age. She has Leukemia."

"Are her parents around?"

"No dad, she has a mom but she works and only comes in the evening for a few hours."

"What's is the young girl's name?"

"Karen and a real cutie."

"Rose, what's up? You seem a little down today."

Rose thought for a second about spinning some story so as to not hurt Bill's feelings, but then decided that the truth was best.

"I had a bad call with Stephanie last night."

"What about?"

"You and Jordan and Golf."

"What about me and Jordan and Golf?"

"She doesn't want Jordan going to the country club. She also isn't crazy about him playing golf. She feels she can't afford to support Jordan playing golf and that none of the kids he associates with play golf, which could isolate Jordan."

"What is wrong with the country club?"

"You know – those labels – rich, white, conservative and" – she stopped herself and Bill finished the sentence.

"Trump." – right?

"Right." Rose confirmed.

There was a long pause with no response from Bill.

Rose asked. "No response?"

Bill responded in his normal calm voice and manner. "OK – I don't understand it. I think Stephanie is wrong. I think she is punishing Jordan. He is her son and if that is what she wants, I will back off."

Bill continued – "you know, if Jordon continues to practice, he could make the high school golf team and maybe even get a college scholarship."

"Stephanie's not sure Jordan has the grades or smarts for college."

"What?" Bill said loudly! "She is wrong about that. He is a smart kid. He just hasn't found his thing yet and golf just might be it."

Rose attempted to soften the tension. "I think Stephanie may change her attitude after a couple days. I will talk to her tonight."

"Well, let me know about tomorrow. I was planning to pick Jordan up at 7 AM. Let me know if that is off."

"OK – I will." Rose replied.

"Hey, I better get back to Karen. Talk to you later." Rose could sense that Bill was annoyed as he left the table. An abrupt exit by Bill, no kiss, no goodbye and it was only 11:45. Rose could feel her world crumbling around her a little bit.

The afternoon seemed to drag on forever. Rose was thinking about Bill, Jordan, Stephanie, etc. There was no communication from Bill. She had texted him around 3 asking if he wanted something from the cafeteria. He responded simply, "no thanks."

At 5:00 she texted Bill again. "Hey, are you getting ready to leave and should I wait for you?"

Bill texted back. "No, don't wait for me, I may be here a while. I will text you later."

Rose went home to her apartment. It seemed cold and empty that night versus the warm, cozy place that it normally was. She wanted to call her daughter, but felt that Stephanie should be calling her. Rose was still upset with what Stephanie had said and how she said it. So, Rose didn't want to make the first move.

When it got to be about 9 PM, Rose couldn't wait any longer and finally called Stephanie to asked about golf tomorrow for Jordan and Bill. Stephanie, said that she had already told Jordan that golf was off for tomorrow. Rose was very upset upon hearing that.

"Stephanie you are punishing your son because of your prejudices. You are depriving him of a good experience and opportunity. This makes no sense."

Stephanie could tell that her mom was upset, but at this point she didn't care. "Mama, he is my son and I have to do what I think is right."

Rose replied – "well, you are wrong and she hung up!" Another hang up without saying goodbye.

She texted Bill and simply said – "no golf with Jordan tomorrow."

Bill responded via text – "OK, Thanks."

Just as Rose was about to respond to Bill's text, her phone buzzed with a call and it was her son Robert. Great, she said out loud, as he never calls unless there is a problem.

Robert started. "Hey mom, how are you?"

"I am fine Robert. How are you? What's up?"

"Mom, I talked to Stephanie today."

Rose got an instant knot in her stomach and asked – "OK, what does that mean?"

"Well, she told me about Bill taking Jordan to the country club and buying him all kinds of golf stuff. Stephanie also told me that she saw Bill watching Fox News with Jordan at your place."

"Robert, that is all true. So, what is the problem?"

"Are you kidding me Mom? You want Jordan exposed to Fox News and all the country club white conservatives and Trump supporters? Is that what you want?"

"Robert, did you ever think what is really best for Jordan or are you just worried about your political agenda? Bill got Jordan outside playing golf, versus sitting around all day playing video games. I think that is a very good thing."

"Mom this is going to be a problem. I agree with Stephanie. I don't think that Bill should be around Jordan alone. Who knows what he is telling him!"

Rose had had enough! "Robert, I am done with this conversation. I will talk to you later. She hung up the phone."

Another tough night for Rose. Her kids were turning on Bill. She was stuck in the middle and Jordan was paying the price. New apartment, new job and new boyfriend but nothing but aggravation. Rose started wondering if her and Bill could just go away if everything would be better? She then remembered that Bill had said that he would text or call her tonight but nothing so far and it was 10PM. Great, she thought.

13 – PILING ON

Rose went in early on Thursday. She wanted to check on Bill so she headed up to 5 as soon as she got there. She no longer cared if people knew that she was checking up on him. She was concerned because he had not heard from him last night. If he was still there and had pulled an all-nighter that would explain the lack of communication from Bill. However, she was worried that the all-nighters were becoming physically difficult for Bill. Again, Rose was feeling like a 65-year-old high school girl.

She got to the reception desk on the 5th floor and luckily for her, she knew the attendant on duty. Loretta, how are you – Rose asked?

I am fine, thanks.

Do you know if Bill is still here?

Hold on Loretta responded. She picked up the phone and was calling someone to check on Bill. Rose assumed it was nurse's station. Loretta hung up and told Rose that he had left about an hour ago. Rose said thanks and headed back to the lobby. She felt relieved that he had been tied up last night and was likely not able to contact her, but also felt bad that he had put in another all-nighter. Rose now assumed that Bill was home sleeping and that she would hear from him later.

It was a normal Thursday at the front reception desk. Rose was feeling better about her issues with Bill and her daughter than she did yesterday.

She wasn't sure why as neither issued had been resolved. After lunch and after the early afternoon rush of visitors, Janet appeared with the quarterly newsletters again. It was early July, so three months since Rose had distributed them in April.

After putting down a big pile of the newsletters on the reception desk Janet, turned to Rose. "Rose you did such a good job at handing these out last time, I thought you might want to do it again.

Rose replied, "sure no problem. Happy to do so." It is a nice change of pace."

Rose turned to Belynda and asked her if she was OK with her leaving the desk and distributing them now. "Sure." Belynda replied. "Have a good time."

So off Rose went on to each level of the hospital putting the newsletter out in every waiting room. It went much faster this time as she knew where she was going and knew most of the people. Her last stop was the 5th floor and she had just finished the 2nd waiting room when Erin the head nurse on the floor called out to her. Rose walked over to see what she wanted.

"Rose, good to see you." The greeting caught Rose a little off guard as they were friendly but had not been very close.

"Good to see you as well." Rose replied.

"Rose, I want to introduce you to Debbie." Erin, pointed to the other nurse in the station. "Debbie just started last week." Debbie said hello and nice to meet you and Rose replied in kind.

Rose noticed that Debbie was very young, probably mid 20's or so and black. She was the first black nurse that she had seen up in the ICU. As Rose was about to walk away, Erin stood up and walked closer to Rose who was standing at the counter.

"Rose, is everything OK with Bill?

Rose immediately knew this was the real reason why Erin called her over.

"As far as I know. Why? He just didn't seem himself yesterday. He was very quiet and seemed down about something."

Rose wasn't sure what to say and she certainly wasn't going to tell Erin about the issue going on with Stephanie, Jordan and Bill.

"I haven't talked to him since lunch yesterday, because he was here all last night."

"Oh, OK – probably nothing." Erin responded and returned to her computer screen.

Rose turned and walked away but feeling like Erin suspected that something was wrong between Bill and her.

Rose got home about 5:30 Thursday evening and still nothing from Bill or Stephanie. After dinner, she was about to call Bill when her phone rang and looking at the caller ID, she saw that it was GG.

"Hey, what's up? Good to hear from you." Rose stated.

"Good to hear from you as well. Is everything OK?"

"Yes, why wouldn't it be?"

"Well, I called Stephanie to talk about the picnic – you know it is tomorrow!"

"I know." Rose responded.

"Well Stephanie said that she hadn't talked to you in few days. That you guys had words and now you weren't talking to her."

"That's not true. We did have words but it's not that I am not talking to her. I just wanted things to calm down before talking to her again."

"What was the argument about? She just said it was about Bill and wouldn't give me any details."

"GG – I don't want to re-hash the issue either. Stephanie said some disrespectful things about Bill to me after he had done her a big favor by watching Jordan for a couple of days. I plan to call her tonight and clear the air."

"That's good because I asked Stephanie if they were coming to the picnic and she said that she thought so but wasn't sure, which surprised me. She also said that she wasn't sure if Robert was coming. I asked her why and she said because of Bill. Rose, what's going on?"

Rose could feel her eyes tearing up but tried to compose herself before answering.

"GG – I am not sure. Bill is the best man that I have ever been with and I love him. But now it is pulling my family apart and I can't understand why? He hasn't done anything to either Steph or Robert – especially not Robert. He has spent almost no time with Bill."

"Rose, I don't know but maybe it is just because he is different."

"You mean because he is white?"

"No, it is not just because he is white. He is also a one percenter, a republican, a conservative and a Trump guy. How can you be with a Trump supporter? He makes everyone, including your children uncomfortable."

"Including you?"

"Yes, including me. Rose, he seems fine when I am with him but I am constantly thinking about all of the other stuff."

Rose was stunned and didn't respond and now was feeling anger starting to build up instead of tears.

GG jumped back in. "Rose, at your age, is this what you want? To tear your family apart over some guy?"

Again, Rose didn't respond immediately.

"GG, I need to think about this. I will talk to Stephanie and let you know if I or we – Bill and me are coming to the picnic or not. Also, Bill is not just some guy." With that, she hung up on GG not saying goodbye.

She was fuming and trying to decide what to do next. Screw it she said to herself and hit the auto-dial for Stephanie.

Stephanie answered. "Hey Mama, good to hear from you." Her tone was friendly and upbeat – sounding like she was trying to forget the tone of the previous call.

"Steph – I just talked to GG. Sounds like you told her about our last call and the issues around Bill." Rose wanting to hear what Stephanie would say.

"Yes Mama, I told her the truth because she asked if I was going to the picnic. I am not sure that I want to go and bring Jordan if Bill is going to be there. I have had a nightmare week with Jordan because of Bill."

"What do you mean?"

"Jordan asks about Bill every day and wants to go golfing with him. He is constantly out back in the courtyard hitting golf balls. He has hit several cars and broke one of my neighbor's windows. He asks about going to the country club and even has mentioned Trump. All because of two days with Bill."

"Oh my God. Rose replied and she had heard enough. "Well, Stephanie, I will make it easy for you and for GG. Bill and I will be at the picnic. If you or anyone else doesn't want to see us or be around us than that is your problem." Again, she hung up the phone without saying goodbye.

Rose was fuming mad and just pacing back and forth, not sure what to do next. Just then her phone buzzed and it was Bill. What a relief she felt seeing his name on the caller ID. "Hello stranger," she said upon answering.

"Hey Rose, sorry about not calling yesterday. I ended up at the hospital all night."

"I know, not a problem."

"I was going to pick us up some fast-food dinner and head over, is that OK?"

"OK. That would be fantastic!"

"Any preference on the food?"

"No, whatever you want is fine."

Bill showed up about a half hour later with Chick Filet, which was one of his favorites.

Over dinner, Rose told Bill about her conversations with GG, Stephanie and Robert. As normal, Bill didn't respond immediately. He always seemed to absorb what he heard and think before talking. This created some awkward pauses, but Rose had learned this process by Bill usually resulted in very thoughtful comments.

Bill started slowly. "Rose, I will do whatever you think is best in regard to the picnic. If you want to go, I will be there. If you don't want to go, I am fine with that. We can have a picnic of our own if you prefer. My only comment is that I don't like being intimidated and judged unfairly."

Rose quickly responded, "me neither. We're going to the picnic!"

After dinner, they watched some TV. Then Rose invited Bill to spend the night which he accepted.

14 – THE HOLIDAY

Bill had decided to play golf the morning of July 4th as the picnic didn't start until Noon. He told Rose that he would pick her up around noon and that they might be a little late to the picnic. She didn't mind at all, saying it didn't really matter when they arrived. He was a little late picking up Rose and didn't get to the picnic until about 12:45.

The picnic was in Elgin Woods. It was a great spot for an outing. Rose's friends and family had been coming here for over 20 years on July 4th. They were able to reserve the Woods location with the city of Elgin each year because Rose's cousin worked for the Elgin Park District. They had plenty of picnic tables, charcoal grills, baseball fields and a large grassy open area.

Pretty much everyone was there when Bill and Rose arrived. Stephanie was the first to approach them and gave her mom a big hug – which Rose appreciated. Stephanie turned and said hello to Bill but no hug or hand shake, which was fine with Bill.

All of a sudden, Jordan came running up. "Hey Bill, how are you?"

Bill quickly reminded him – "Jordan, don't you say hello to your grandma?"

With that, he turned to Rose and gave her a hug. "Hi Grandma."

Jordan then asked Bill to join him saying that he wanted to show him something. "Where are we going?" Bill asked.

"You'll see." Jordan replied.

Off they went, heading to the open grassy area.

Rose didn't say anything but gave Stephanie a look that said – oh yeah – what a terrible thing that's going on between Bill and Jordan.

Rose started walking around saying hello to old family and friends. Everyone was happy to see her. Some asked about Bill and some didn't. She finally ran into Robert who had not gone out of his way to find Rose. She gave him a hug and kiss and said hello. He responded with the same but didn't ask about Bill, which Rose didn't expect.

"Good to see you, son. How have you been?"

"Good to see you too, Mom. I have been fine."

"Let's have a good day today. OK?" That was code for behave yourself.

"That's the plan Mom. Time to play some softball." Robert stated very loudly in an attempt to get the game going and end an uncomfortable discussion with his mother.

With that, Robert yelled out – "SOFTBALL TIME EVERYONE!"

Most of the guys and some of girls started heading for the softball field. Rose and others not planning to play headed back over to the tables and grills to start cooking. Lunch was normally right after the softball game ended. Robert seemed to be the organizer of the game trying to create two even teams. Robert yelled out to Stephanie – "where's Jordan? Get Jordan!"

Stephanie looked around and saw that Jordan was with Bill in the grassy field hitting golf balls. She started walking that way and called out to Jordan.

"Jordan – let's go. It is time for the softball game." Jordan didn't respond and Bill didn't hear Stephanie calling him.

Finally, Stephanie got up next to Bill and Jordan. "Jordan, it's time for the softball game. Let's go."

"Mom, I don't want to play. I am golfing with Bill."

"Jordan, your uncle wants you to play. You play every year and all the other kids are playing."

Bill tried to help. "Jordan, that's OK. We can golf more when the game is over."

"No – I don't want to play softball!"

Stephanie gave Bill a look and headed back over to the field to give Robert the news. Bill was watching and he could see that Robert was not happy and giving her a bad time. Robert looked toward Bill and shot some long-range eye daggers at him! As Bill watched, Stephanie made a beeline to her mother and was giving Rose an earful. Bill knew that he would be hearing about this.

Bill and Jordan went back to hitting balls and the softball game started. After about an hour, Bill noticed Rose walking their way. Bill walked to meet her halfway. "Time to eat." Rose stated.

Bill asked, "am I in trouble again?"

"Oh yeah.", Rose replied.

Bill turned and yelled to Jordan, "time for lunch. Let's go." Jordan dropped his clubs and started to come. Bill yelled back at Jordan – "whoa. Jordan, get your clubs and bag and bring them with you." Jordan did as Bill asked.

They sat down for lunch. Bill, Rose and Jordan sitting by themselves at one of the picnic tables.

Bill could feel the eyes on him and could hear Robert and Stephanie still going at it with their voices getting louder. He could also tell that Robert was feeling no pain from a few too many beers.

After lunch, Jordan wanted Bill to go back and hit balls with him. Bill told him that he had to help cleanup and would join him later. Bill turned to start helping and Robert was standing there.

"Hey, Robert – how are you doing?"

"Not good, Robert said. What are you doing?"

"I am helping clear the tables. Is that the question?"

"Very funny. It's more than that – much more. You are impacting our family, inserting your life into ours, and planting ideas into Jordan! Who told you that would be, OK?"

Bill paused for a second. "Nobody told me it was OK, but I have never asked permission to do the right thing."

"Like voting for Trump was that the right thing?"

Suddenly, there were two other men standing next to them listening.

"Yes, I think it was the right thing to do."

Robert clearly growing agitated and the crowd seemed to be growing steadily.

"That makes you a racist, like Trump."

"I don't agree about me or Trump!"

Bill was reading the crowd and he could tell that the he was clearly not winning them over.

Just then Rose appeared next to them. "What are you guys talking about?"

Robert spoke first. "Bill was just telling us what a big fan of Trump that he is."

"What. Why?" Rose asked as she turned toward Bill.

"Because he asked me." Bill responded. With that, Rose took him by the hand and led him away.

As they were walking, Rose asked – "Bill, why would you talk politics here?"

"I didn't plan to or want to Rose, but your son asked me?"

"He was just trying to get your goat! He wanted to get you to say something about Trump."

"I know that but I was not going to lie. He asked me a direct question and I gave him a direct answer. Remember what I said about labels, Rose?"

"I know but today is not the day. You shouldn't let him get to you like that."

Bill stopped walking and turned to look directly at Rose. "You know what, I am going to go. Robert or Stephanie can give you a ride home. I need to stop by the hospital anyway."

As Bill started to walk toward his car, Rose grabbed his arm. "Bill please wait a second. I didn't mean anything, I am sorry."

Bill interrupted her. "Rose, it's OK, I will call you later."

The picnic was a disaster. Jordan was upset that Bill left and wouldn't talk to anyone. Stephanie thought that the confrontation between Robert and Bill was Bill's fault.

Rose asked GG for a ride home, because she didn't want to be with her daughter or son. She knew that was a terrible thing to think but that is what she was feeling. GG didn't say much on the way home – which Rose appreciated. However, GG did suggest that Rose just cool it for a while in regard to her relationship with Bill.

Rose got home and just sat in the dark and cried. She never felt more alone. She wanted to call Bill in the worst way but decided to take GG's advice and just let things settle tonight. She expected to see Bill tomorrow at Delnor and would talk to him face to face. Crap, she thought, today is Friday – so no work tomorrow. She would simply call Bill first thing Saturday morning.

15 – ALONE TIME

Rose didn't sleep much Friday night with her thoughts bouncing between Bill and her children, but mostly Bill. She was up early in anticipation of calling Bill. She knew that he was almost certainly up, but didn't want to call this early as it wasn't even 7AM yet. At 8AM, she couldn't wait any longer. She called Bill's cell and it went directly to voice mail. She decided not to leave a voice mail. Great, she thought. It was sunny out so she assumed that he was golfing.

Rose fell back on her previous normal Saturday routine. She cleaned her apartment from top to bottom. Then she went food shopping and dropped off her clothes at the dry cleaner. Also, picking up the clothes that she had dropped off last week. By the time she got back home, it was about noon. She called Bill again and got his voice mail again – crap, she exclaimed out loud. So, she sent him a text. "Hey, give me a call when you get a chance - love, Rose."

Finally, about 2 in the afternoon her phone buzzed and it was a text from Bill. Hey – had a chance to go up to Kohler with some golf buddies for a weekend of golf. Will be back late Sunday. Talk to you then.

That message did not feel good to Rose. He hadn't mentioned going away this weekend. Also, if he wanted to talk to her, she thought that he could find time to do so. What the heck? So, she texted back. "Thanks for the update – I really would like to talk to you before Sunday night."

She got an immediate text answer from Bill. "OK, I will call you later." It will probably be around 6PM.

That message made Rose feel better and gave her some hope that she wouldn't be waiting all weekend to talk to him. Rose spent the next 4 hours cleaning, reading and even took a nap to make up for her restless night of limited sleep.

As promised, Bill called about 6 PM.

Rose answered. "Hey Bill, how are you?"

"Good. Just finished our afternoon round of golf, took a shower and about to head out to dinner with the guys."

"When did this trip come about? You never mentioned it."

"It was a last-minute thing. My friend John called last night and asked if I was interested in going. One of their guys dropped out at the last minute."

"Oh – OK. Where are you staying up there? I have never been to Kohler but heard good things."

"We are at the American Club. The only five-star and five-diamond hotel in Wisconsin."

"Wow, really – it must be nice."

"It is."

Rose realized that she was dancing around the issue that she really wanted to talk about.

"Bill, I just wanted to talk about what happened yesterday at the picnic. I wasn't blaming you for what happened. I know how Robert can be and I was just embarrassed and said the wrong thing."

"Rose, this is something that we should probably discuss in person and not over the phone. However, I will say that this is more than just what happened at the picnic. Your children obviously do not want me around. It is going to be hard for us to have a relationship with that hanging over us.

It is impacting your relationship with your children and grandson and that is unacceptable."

"Bill, I am not worried about that. I can handle my children."

"OK – let's talk on Monday. I am not getting back until late Sunday night. We can talk at the hospital on Monday or after work if you prefer."

"OK, Bill. "Have a good time golfing and be careful."

"Thanks, Rose. Bye."

Rose was glad that they talked, but was not at all thrilled with the tone of the conversation. It was just more stuff to think about. She wanted to talk to somebody in the worst way, but had no one to call. For the first time since she started seeing Bill, she was having doubts about the relationship.

She was 65 years old and Bill was 70 – so where was this going long term? They had separate families and they were never going to come together. There are just too many differences. At her age, she thought she would be spending more time with her children and grandchildren, but now the opposite was happening.

Rose was wondering if she had moved too fast with Bill. It was probably because her marriage had been broken for a long time before it ended. Maybe she got carried away because a nice guy showed a romantic interest in her for the first time in a really long time. She didn't stop to consider the impact on others around her.

It now felt like she was talking herself into a decision that she didn't want to make. She decided to stop thinking about it for now. She watched a movie and went to bed. Tomorrow is Sunday and maybe going to church will help.

Sunday morning Rose headed to church as normal. Today was Donut Sunday. She ran into Stephanie, Jordan and GG in the activity center after the service. The donuts and coffee are free so it was always well attended. Especially by those families with children. They all got their donuts and drinks and sat down at one of the long cafeteria style tables.

As soon as Jordan sat down next to Rose he asked – "Grandma, where's Bill?" Rose told him that Bill was golfing and wouldn't back until later today. It was obvious from the looks on the faces of Stephanie and GG that just the mention of Bill was creating anxiety.

Not wanting to talk about Bill in front of Jordan, Rose turned to Jordan. "Honey if you are done with your donut, why don't you go to the playground outside with the other kids."

Jordan replied – "Grandma I am a little old for the playground."

"Well then just go outside for a while because I want to talk to your mom and GG."

"OK." Jordan replied, and off he went.

Rose then turned to Stephanie and GG and started. "Look, I have some things to say. I have been thinking about what happened at the picnic on Friday and how my relationship with Bill is impacting everyone."

"Mama." Stephanie tried to jump in but Rose cut her off.

"Wait, let me finish. I am planning to pause or end my relationship with Bill. It will probably be when I see him tomorrow at the hospital. This is the hardest thing that I have ever done. It is much worse than when I divorced your father - Stephanie. I love Bill and he has been nothing but great to me and my family. But – it is splitting our family apart."

"Mama, you have only known him for what – 3 or 4 months. You don't really know him. How can you say that you love him? Have you spent any time with his sons – no – why not? Has he taken you to the country club – no – why not? Have you met any of his friends or family – no – why not? You see him at the hospital and a couple of times each week and that's it. There's a lot you don't know about him. Mama, I just don't want you to get hurt."

Stephanie continued. "Mama, your relationship with Dad was not very good for many years. So now, you fall for the first guy that shows an interest in you. That is natural – like a rebound from a bad relationship. Also, I am not saying that he is a bad guy but very different from us. Given his background, I just don't trust him."

"Stephanie, while I appreciate your concern, you are wrong. Yes, I have only been dating him for 3 or 4 months. However, that was a close and personal 3 to 4 months. I have been to the country club, I have met his sons, we have spent a fair amount of personal time together, we have traveled together and I have seen him in very personal and stressful situations. So, I do think that I know him pretty well."

"GG finally spoke up. "Rose, I feel like I am piling on a little, but I agree with Stephanie that you don't know him yet. In spite of the time that you have spent together. Plus, he is really different than we are. Not just his race but everything else – you know what I mean. That doesn't make him a bad guy but somebody you don't know. I am not saying you should break up with him, but like I said the other day, take a pause and let things quiet down for a while. Maybe see some other people. If he is Mr. Right and you two are meant to be together, then it will happen."

Rose sat there without responding. She knew in her heart that she loved Bill. However, some of what they were saying was true. She has only known him from a brief time. Also, he does live in a different world and one that is vastly different than the one she comes from. She also knew that there would be no pausing the relationship with Bill. Rose was the first woman that he had any kind of relationship with since his wife died. She knew Bill was all in with her. If he thought she didn't feel the same, then he would simply walk away. He would view it as a betrayal and she knew it.

Stephanie spoke again since her mother was not saying anything. "Mama, have you spoken to Robert since the picnic?"

Rose replied in a stern tone. "No - I have not."

"He feels badly about what happened and about how it embarrassed you."

"Maybe he should call me and say that!"

"I know, I told him the same thing. He said that he would call you today, but he doesn't want to be around Bill. He simply sees Bill as a one-per-center Trump country club guy."

"Labels." Rose said out loud.

"What?" Stephanie asked?

"Nothing." Rose replied.

Rose had heard enough. "OK ladies, I need to think about this and decide what I am going to do before tomorrow. I will probably end it or pause it or something. That seems to be the best course of action and what everyone wants. Who was I kidding, a 65-year-old grandmother trying to have a relationship. Stupid."

Rose grabbed her purse and started to walk away without saying goodbye. "Mama." Stephanie called out but Rose just kept walking.

Rose tried to keep herself busy the rest of the day. She went to the Woodfield Mall which is one of the largest in the country and always crowded. It has 3 or 4 levels and has about every store and restaurant that exists. She spent hours there, window shopping and then decided to treat herself to a new dress from Nordstrom. Normally she would not buy clothes or anything else from Nordstrom as it was out of her price range. She was depressed and figured what the hell! The thought of looking nice for Bill also flashed through her mind, but then she caught herself – look nice for the guy you are planning to dump, that makes a lot of sense.

After buying the dress, she had dinner in the food court. It was not great – fast food Chinese – but she didn't want to cook when she returned home. It was 6 PM by the time she got home. She checked her phone and there were two texts from Stephanie and one from GG asking how she was doing and to give them a call if she wanted to talk – which she didn't.

The rest of the night was torture. She tried to read, watch TV and even do a 1,000-piece puzzle, but nothing could take her mind off of talking to Bill tomorrow. She thought that maybe he would text or call her tonight when he returned from Kohler but nothing. Rose went to bed early and stared at the ceiling for a while before falling asleep.

16 – CRAP

Rose woke up early on Monday and decided that she would go into the hospital a little early. She also wanted to be sure that she got there before Bill so she wouldn't miss him when he arrived. As soon as she pulled into the parking garage, she noticed two Kane County Sheriff vehicles parked in the first row in the handicap spots. The cars were empty so she assumed that something was going on.

As she walked from the parking garage into the main lobby, the county policemen were standing at each entrance and by the elevator bank. The was also another police car parked by the front entrance. She walked to the reception desk where Belynda was already on duty.

"Morning Belynda, what is going on with all the police"

"One of their prisoners is up in the ICU. Normally that means that he got stabbed by another inmate."

"When did they arrive?"

"Not sure, they were here when I arrived about 30 minutes ago."

Belynda then noticed Rose's new dress. "Rose, I love your dress, is that new?"

"Yes, I bought it yesterday."

"What's the occasion?"

"Nothing, just felt like getting a new dress."

"Good for you."

"Have you seen Bill come in yet?

"No, not yet – wait, here he comes now."

Rose turned around to see him talking to one of the deputy sheriffs.

Bill then headed over to the reception desk. "Morning Rose, morning Belynda. Hey Rose, you look good - nice dress."

Belynda and Rose both returned a good morning. Rose came out from behind the desk so she could have a little privacy. "Thanks, Bill. How was golf?"

"Golf was great. So, you haven't you been up to Kohler?"

"No, but I have heard good things. Bill, are you free for lunch?"

"Yes, I will be there at noon."

"Good, I want to talk about some things – you know – the 4th and my children." She could tell that Bill was reading her face and eyes.

Bill just came out and asked her – "Rose are you breaking up with me?" Rose was startled by Bill's directness and hadn't expected Bill to go there so fast.

'No, not breaking up. I just think that maybe we should" – and she stopped herself. "Bill, I would rather wait until lunch so we have more time to talk and a better setting."

Bill didn't respond immediately. He just stared right through her. Finally, he replied. "OK, I have to go, see you later." He turned away and off he went to take the elevator to the 5th floor. Rose watched him hoping that he would look back but he didn't.

Rose returned back to the reception desk and she felt like she was going to pass out. The feeling of dread was overwhelming. She had blown it with Bill. She knew that he could see through her and she knew that there would be no middle ground. In spite of what everyone was saying she didn't care. She didn't want to break up or stop seeing him or put anything on pause.

She immediately pulled out her phone and texted Bill – "Sorry – can't wait to see you at lunch, Love – Rose."

Belynda noticed something wasn't right. "Rose, what's up?" Belynda thinking something may be wrong with Bill.

"Oh nothing. Just some family stuff." Rose did not want to get into the gory details.

About that time, the morning rush started and Rose was pretty busy. Janet came out to tell Rose and Belynda that because of the prisoner on 5 in the ICU, no visitors could go up to the 5th floor.

Belynda asked – "for how long?"

"They expect him to be released this afternoon. Until he is gone, no visitors are allowed." Janet replied in a very authoritative tone.

"Janet, Bill just went up to 5. Is that OK?" Rose asked.

"Yes. Bill is not a visitor and anyway, he will be in the cancer side of the 5th floor."

By about 11:30 things at the desk had settled down. Rose checked her phone to see if Bill had responded to her text but nothing. As she was starting to clean up her area, she heard talking on all of the police radios. It was like stereo because there were 4 deputies in the lobby.

SHOTS FIRED, SHOTS FIRED, MAN DOWN! All four deputes pulled their guns. One of them yelled cover the exits. Nobody in or out – Lockdown! With that a loud alarm went off. It was different than the fire alarm, a new alarm sound that Rose had not heard before.

"What is that?" Rose asked Belynda?

"That is the lockdown alarm. It means that there is an active shooter in the building."

The phone at the desk rang. It was Janet telling Belynda that she and Rose needed to come into the office and into the large conference room. During a lockdown, the plan was for the office staff to go into the conference room and literally lock the door.

ON THE 5TH FLOOR there was chaos –

When Bill arrived in the morning, he had noticed an unarmed hospital security guard in the 5th floor lobby. He also noticed an armed sheriff's deputy standing outside one of the ICU rooms. He assumed that room was where the prisoner was getting treatment. As he walked past the ICU nurse's desk, he waved to Erin and Debbie. Both waved back with Erin rolling her eyes about the special visitor.

Bill didn't have any one patient that needed his attention. He was going from room to room on the cancer side of the floor - spending about 20 minutes with each patient. His plan was to spend the morning on the 5th floor and then the afternoon in the CC on the first floor.

He had just sat down with Maria Gomez who had just had surgery to remove a cancerous tumor in her abdomen, when he heard yelling and then the distinctively loud sound of two gunshots – POP! – POP!

Bill rushed out of Maria's room and headed toward the cancer ward nurses station. He tried the hallway side door into the station, but it was closed and locked. He walked around to the window on the front of the station and couldn't see anybody. He looked over at the ICU nurse's station and it was empty as well.

He then noticed that the sheriff was no longer standing outside the door of the room where the prisoner was located. "What the hell is going on?" He said out-loud.

He heard a voice behind him from the cancer ward nurse's station. "Bill, get in here." It was Carolyn one of the cancer nurses, she had been crouched down below the window so nobody could see her. Bill looked over the edge and saw another nurse and one of the cancer doctors.

Bill wondered why the hospital security guard hadn't come in to help. He walked over to the lobby and looked through the glass doors and there was nobody there. What the heck, he again said out loud. Things seemed to be moving in slow motion. Bill knew that he had been running from spot to spot because he was breathing hard.

He then heard yelling and screams from down the hallway. He got to the ICU room where the sheriff's deputy had been standing and he could hear Erin pleading – stop please don't.

With that Bill opened the door. The door only opened a few feet and was hitting up against something. He looked down and saw the deputy on the floor and saw that he had been shot and probably killed. With that he gave a hard push against the door which moved the deputy's legs back enough to allow Bill to enter the room.

Erin was on the floor holding her head with blood running down her face. The prisoner was attempting to push Debbie down on the bed and pull her clothes off at the same time. Luckily for Bill, the prisoner had set the gun down on the bed. He was using both hands to try to control Debbie. The prisoner saw Bill enter and reached for the gun with his right hand. Bill rushed him and got to him just as he was lifting the gun to point it at Bill. Bill grabbed the prisoner's right hand that was holding the gun with both of his hands.

As Bill and the prisoner began to wrestle for the gun, Debbie fell to the floor next to Erin. She had not been assaulted but was pretty traumatized. As Bill continued to fight for the gun, he realized that in spite of the prisoner's injuries, he was no match for the younger and stronger man. It was a matter of time before he lost control of the weapon. At that time, he launched his knee into the crotch of the prisoner, which definitely weaken his opponent and thrust him back against the wall.

The prisoner's arm that was holding the gun was straight down, but Bill could feel him bending his arm and hand attempting to bring the gun up and point it at Bill. Bill then slid his hands down the gun from the handle to the barrel. This allowed Bill to turn and twist the gun and try to get it out of the prisoner's grip. As this was going on, Bill heard two more shots – even louder than before – POP! – POP!

As Bill was twisting the gun barrel, the prisoner could feel that he was losing control and was able to move this finger to the trigger and pull it twice. The first bullet hit Bill in the lower left hip. The second came straight up between the two men and struck the prisoner under the chin and through the top of his head. The bullet blew the top of his head off and killed him instantly. The prisoner collapsed with Bill falling down on top of him and hitting his head very-hard on the marble window sill as he was falling.

BACK ON THE FIRST floor, the lock down continued with the alarm continuing to sound. In the locked conference room, the office personnel couldn't hear anything and didn't really know what was going on. They heard someone running through the office and they stopped at the locked door. The person yelled – "Sheriff's deputy, are you guys OK in there?"

Janet responded. "Yes, can we come out?"

The deputy responded with an emphatic "No. There have just been more shots fired up on the 5th floor."

With that news there was a notable gasp from everyone in the room. Up to this point, Rose hadn't been concerned about Bill, because she figured that he was in lockdown just like they were. Now however for the first time she began to worry. She checked her phone and no call or text from Bill.

Rose made her way from the back of the crowded conference room over to where Janet was standing. She touched Janet's arm to turn her around.

"Janet – can we call up to the nurse's station on 5 to make sure that everyone is - OK?"

"Rose – I don't know. I don't think we should. It must chaos up there right now."

"You're right." Rose replied.

Janet could see in Rose's eyes that she was breaking down and knew that she was worried about Bill. "Let's wait 5 minutes, if we don't hear anything, I will call."

"Ok."

Rose stayed right next to Janet, continuously checking the time on her phone. After 5 minutes, she touched Janet on the arm again. "OK, I will call." Janet said. "We need to use the internal phone." As Janet and Rose were making their way through the overcrowded room to where the internal phone was located, her cell rang. The caller ID was Delnor Hospital.

Janet answered – "Hello." Everyone in the conference room was talking and Janet couldn't hear what the person on the phone was saying. She pressed the phone against her stomach and yelled – "please quiet down. I have a phone call." She returned the phone to her ear. "Sorry – hello. Oh, we were just about to call you. OK, yes, she is here – OK – oh my God – OK – OK - I will tell her." Rose already figured that something was wrong on the 5th floor and that it was something with Bill.

Before Janet could tell her, Rose had put both hands on Janet's shoulders asking her "what - what?"

Janet replied. "Rose, Bill has been shot." The words hit Rose like a hard slap in the face.

Rose immediately bolted for the door just pushing people aside. Janet and Belynda went after her. Janet was yelling – "Rose, wait - where are you going, we are still on lockdown." The alarm was still sounding.

"I don't care I am going up to 5."

"He's not there." Janet shouted!

Rose stopped and asked – "where is he?"

They are taking him down to surgery, Erin is with him and will meet us there.

Hearing that, Rose was out the door with Janet and Belynda following.

UP ON 5 –

The ICU hospital room looked like a war zone. There was blood from the deputy being shot as he had bled out, his blood was all over the floor. The shot that went through the prisoner's head had splatted blood over the windows, ceiling and everything and everyone else in the room. Bill had fallen and severely cracked his head on the window sill and was bleeding profusely from his head and the gunshot wound to his hip. Erin was also bleeding badly from her head as the result of being pistol whipped by the prisoner when he made his escape.

In spite of her injuries, Erin reacted quickly. She rolled Bill over. He was not conscious so Erin checked his pulse which was still strong but she knew he was losing a lot of blood. She immediately put pressure on the gunshot wound to slow down the bleeding. She told Debbie to hit her code blue button. Last year Delnor installed a wireless code blue system in the ICU. Each nurse wore a pager like a button that she could hit that sounded a code blue alarm and provided the room number to the doctors and nurses.

Within seconds the doctors and nurses that had been locked down on the 5th floor started to arrive and assist. At the same time, the sheriff's police arrived with their guns drawn bursting into the room. It was a very chaotic scene as the sheriff was concerned about their officer and wanted to make sure that the prisoner was secure. Erin and the doctors knew that they had only minutes to get Bill down to surgery before he died.

Erin and the doctor were yelling at the police to move their man who was obviously deceased. They needed to get Bill out ASAP. The officers did as they were instructed. They then rushed to lift Bill out of the room and onto a gurney. Erin, Debbie and the doctor then rushed Bill to the back elevator that goes directly down to surgery.

While they were pushing the gurney to the elevator the doctor was talking into her wireless mic to have the emergency surgeon waiting. Erin could see Bill's breathing shallowing out. She knew that they had only a few minutes to save his life.

17 – THE BATTLE

Janet led Rose the back way to the operating waiting room through the office area. As a result of the lockdown all scheduled operations had been cancelled. The operating area was empty and everyone and everything was focused on Bill. By the time Rose, Janet and Belynda arrived Bill was in surgery.

There are three areas in the surgery unit, which is referred to as the OR by the hospital staff. The first area in the OR is the visitor waiting area. The next area is the surgery prep area where patients scheduled for surgery are prepared and evaluated by nurses. The third area are the surgery rooms themselves. Delnor has five surgery rooms which were never all used at the same time. One had to always be left available for emergencies.

When Rose arrived to the waiting area, she was frantic to find out what was happening. She tried to enter the prep area from the waiting room, but that door was always kept locked. Rose knocked and then pounded but no answer. Finally, after a few minutes, Erin emerged followed by doctor Dr. Schengel who had helped Erin with Bill in the ICU.

The site of Erin was horrific for Rose to see. Erin was covered in blood from head to foot including a large wound on her forehead. Even worse for Rose, she assumed that it was Bill's blood all over Erin. Rose's knees weakened and she collapsed to the ground. "Oh my God, oh my god." Rose kept repeating. "Is that blood from Bill, she asked Erin."

Belynda and Janet went down to Rose to comfort her and help get her back up into a chair. Erin came over and apologized to Rose for her appearance and stated that she had just pushed Bill into the surgery room. Erin ignored Rose's question as to whether the blood on her nurse's gown was from Bill – but a lot of it was.

As Erin started talking to Rose, Dr. Schengel was holding her arm and trying to pull her back into the OR for treatment of her wound. However, Erin knew that she had to give Rose an update on Bill.

Erin began – "Rose, he is in surgery. He literally just went into the OR. Dr. Samuel, the chief surgeon of Delnor is treating Bill. He is getting the best care possible. It is going to be a while, probably hours. You need to just wait and make whatever calls you need to make to Bill's family."

Erin had decided not to give Rose the details of Bill's injuries. However, Rose wasn't having that. "Erin, what's his condition? What are his injuries?"

Erin knew that she had no choice. "Rose, he has a gunshot wound to his left hip and a severe blow to the head, and he has lost a lot of blood. His condition is extremely critical."

With that update, Rose put her head into her hand crying uncontrollably. Erin could see that Rose was losing it so continued to talk to get Rose's attention and calm her down.

"Rose, you should also know that Bill saved Debbie and me from a monster! We owe him our lives."

Belynda then asked, "what happened to the monster?"

Erin hesitated gathering her thoughts. "He's dead! Bill killed him. Thank God."

Those words hung in the air for a minute, catching everyone off guard.

Dr. Schengel jumped in and said, "ladies – I need to treat Erin's injuries now." She then started to guide Erin back into the OR prep area. However, then Rose stood up and walked over to Erin and wrapped both arms around her and whispered into her ear – "Thank You – I know that you saved him." They then exchanged a parting glance and Erin proceeded back into the OR.

Rose feeling like she was going to faint, sat back in her chair attempting to compose herself. She then closed her eyes and folded her hands to say a prayer. Belynda and Janet were next to her providing comfort and making sure that she was OK. As Rose was praying, she couldn't help but think about the last conversation that she had that morning with Bill. He had read her thoughts and comments and believed that Rose was breaking up with him. That was his last thought about Rose when he faced all of this and was shot. Maybe she was somewhat responsible entered her mind as crazy as that sounds.

I have to call Bill's sons and my kids and let them know what is going on. Luckily, Rose had both of Bill's sons contact info and was able to reach them. They said that they were on their way. She also texted Stephanie and provided her with an update. She also said that she was coming and would let Robert know what happened. She closed her phone and checked the time, it was 1:30 PM and this whole episode had only been a couple of hours so far.

About that time two sheriff deputies arrived in the waiting room. One sat down just inside the entrance and the other stood in the front next to the door into the OR. Given all that had gone on at the hospital today, this was a little unnerving. Why were they here, was there a threat or another problem? Belynda decided to find out. She approached the deputy standing at the front of the room.

"Why are you guys here?" Is there another problem?

"No." The deputy replied. "We are simply taking a pre-caution." Belynda could tell that the deputy was not going to provide much info, but she asked him one more time. "A pre-caution for what?"

"It is just a show of police presence. We also have men stationed in lobby and still have our vehicles parked out front. We just want the patients and visitors to feel safe."

With that, Belynda walked back over to Rose and sat down next to her. She didn't want to alarm her so she told Rose that it was nothing. Belynda sat there thinking that it was likely more about protecting Bill from the friends and relatives of the guy that Bill had killed.

People now started to arrive into the waiting room. Stephanie was first to arrive. She hugged her mom and tears flowed from both of them. Stephanie also saying that she was sorry. Rose wasn't exactly sure what she was apologizing for, but now was not the time to ask.

Bill's sons both arrived at about the same time. Both came up to Rose and gave her a hug and started to ask questions about how their dad was doing and what had happened. Rose told them what she knew – which wasn't a lot at this point. Stephanie, Belynda and Janet - all introduced themselves to Matthew and David and all three received a hug from the boys. This was the first sign to Stephanie that Bill's sons were not quite what she expected.

Everyone took a seat as there was nothing to do except to wait. Matthew and David continued to discuss what had happened with each other wondering where the police and security guards were when all this was happening. Janet came over to where the boys were sitting and asked them to calm down as now was not the right time or place for this discussion. The boys agreed and sat back and waited.

About the time, Jim Bradley, the Kane County Sheriff arrived. He had just come from the ICU on the 5th floor. He updated Rose and Bill's sons on what had transpired in that ICU room earlier that afternoon. The Sheriff stated that they didn't really know yet how the prisoner had taken the gun from one of his deputies, but that it had cost him his life. However, it was obvious that Mr. Campbell had likely saved several lives by overpowering the prisoner. "Just going into that room and confronting an armed prisoner requires unique bravery," the Sheriff explained. The Sheriff then explained that he was going to keep deputies posted around Bill – just in case. With that, the Sheriff gave each of them his card and said to call if they needed anything. He then excused himself and left the waiting room.

The magnitude of what Bill had done washed over everyone. They all sat down and began the waiting process.

Janet told Rose that she had to go check on things up front. She knew that both of her receptionists were in the waiting room and had to make sure that somebody was manning the lobby reception desk. She also wanted to check on the office personnel that she hadn't seen since she left the conference room with Rose a couple of hours ago.

When she got to the lobby, she was relieved to see that Katie was at the desk. There was still a strong police presence with a lot of deputies and county personnel going to and from the elevators. Janet thanked Katie for jumping in to cover the desk. Katie said that she had also called Gary and asked him to come in early. Janet thanked her for doing that and thought to herself – wow, Katie really stepped up.

Katie then asked Janet – "how is Bill, how is Rose?" Janet replied – "Bill is still in surgery and Rose is waiting in the OR." Bill's sons and Rose's daughter are there now as well.

"Janet, do you know what happened up in the ICU?" Janet relayed what the Sheriff had just told them and Katie replied with a WOW.

Janet then asked Katie what was going on now - upstairs in the ICU? Katie replied, "it is a crime scene. There is a ton of police up there and the coroner. I have heard that they have had to move some of the ICU patients down into the cancer side of the 5th floor. They told me, no visitors to the 5th floor until they say differently."

"OK – thanks Katie. Let me know if you need anything. I am heading back to the office and then back to OR waiting room. Call my cell if you need anything."

"Will do." Katie replied.

When Janet walked back into the OR waiting room, Erin was entering from the OR prep area through the door at the front of the room. Perfect timing, she thought. It was now 3:00 and they had not gotten any update since Bill went into surgery.

By the time Janet got to the front of the room, Erin was surrounded. Rose, her daughter, Bill's sons and Belynda were all standing. Erin looked much better than the last time that they saw her. She had showered and changed clothes and her head wound was now bandaged. Erin's message was brief saying that Bill was still in surgery and that it would still be a while. She also noted that Bill would likely need an MRI or CT scan on his head soon after surgery. She didn't know if it would literally be immediately after surgery or would be tomorrow. That would be up to the surgeon.

Erin's message was relatively brief. She then told Rose that she had to get back up to the ICU as they were having to move patients, because of the police investigation. She mentioned that future updates would be coming from Karen, the head OR nurse or the surgeon.

Everyone had just sat back down and started the agonizing process of waiting again when Rose's son Robert came through the door into the waiting area. He made a direct line to Rose and gave her a big hug and just like Stephanie - said he was sorry. Rose could tell he was feeling guilty and held the embrace telling Robert – "it's OK, I am glad you are here."

After Robert was done hugging his mother and composed himself, Rose introduced Robert to Bill's sons – Matthew and David. Robert then went to sit next to Stephanie and she gave him hug as well – saying "thank you." She was very happy that Robert had made the effort to support their mother.

Rose was sitting there thinking about all the commotion and conversation that had gone on over the past week and how that all now seemed meaningless and forgotten. Except, she couldn't forget her exchange with Bill this morning before he went upstairs. She was praying that Bill had forgotten their discussion wasn't thinking that she wanted to break up with him. If he did, she would never forgive herself.

About that time Rose noticed an older black couple coming into the waiting area. They also caught the attention of the deputy sheriff as well as he immediately stood up and put his hand on his holstered gun. Rose wasn't sure who they were but then saw Debbie the ICU nurse from upstairs. The couple stopped and let Debbie come forward. Rose assumed that they were Debbie's parents.

Rose remembered what Erin had said earlier about Bill saving her and Debbie's life. Rose didn't know the details that the prisoner was in the process of trying to assault Debbie when Bill stepped in.

When Debbie got to Rose, she just broke down and hugged Rose who had stood up to meet her. Debbie's knees were weak and Rose was having to use all of her strength to help Debbie stand. Her parents rushed in and tried to explain that Debbie was a wreck about what happened. They didn't want her to come but she wanted to be there for Bill. Nobody else could understand what was happening. Rose was able to comfort and calm Debbie and just continued to hold her. Debbie wanted to explain to Rose how Bill had saved her. Rose cut her off saying that Erin had told her. Rose didn't want Debbie to have to re-live the incident in front of everybody. Rose then told Debbie that she wanted to introduce her to some people.

With that, Rose introduced Debbie to Bill's sons. She started crying again as she hugged each of them. Debbie continued to repeat how Bill had saved her. Her parents also hugged the boys, thanking them.

Debbie and her parents were black and seeing them hug Bill's sons was an interesting scene. This scene and its significance, was not lost on Stephanie and Robert, who were standing close by.

After all of this finally calmed down and Debbie and her parents took a seat, Rose checked her phone and it was 5:30. Bill had been in surgery for about 4 hours. She noticed that Belynda and Janet were both still there. She went to both of them and told them that they didn't need to stay. They both had families and needed to get home to them. Both said not a problem because they had texted their families and they knew where they were. Both knew that they had to stay in case things went the wrong way with Bill. They had to be there for Rose - just in case.

At that time, the door to the OR opened and a doctor in a surgical gown walked out. He introduced himself as Doctor John Samuel. Since there were a lot people in the room, he wasn't sure who exactly he should be addressing. He asked, if everyone there was connected with Bill? He got a combined yes from the group.

"OK, good. Please sit down. The surgery is over and Bill is stable. He remains in critical condition and will require additional surgeries, but for now he is stable. Bill was lucky in that the gun must have been at an angle when it went off." The doctor put his hand in the form of a gun in front of his left hip to show what he was talking about. "The bullet entered on his left side. As a result of the gun angle the bullet didn't penetrate directly in or up into his mid-section. The bullet struck his hip and therefore missed his vital organs. It went through his left hip and exited out his back side."

"The hip was broken which sounds bad, but that is much better than being shattered into a thousand pieces. We were able to put his hip back together with pins. He will require additional surgeries and a fair amount of rehab to enable him to walk again."

Bill also sustained a very substantial head trauma that required 50 plus stitches to close. He almost certainly has a severe concussion. There is also a chance that he may have some swelling and internal bleeding in his head. He is on his way right now for an CT scan on his brain to let us know. If there is bleeding or swelling, we will have to put him back into surgery to address that issue.

Dr. Samuel continued, "where do we go from here? After the scan – if his head looks OK, Bill will be in recovery for an hour or two. He will then go up to ICU for rest. He has lost a lot of blood and requires time to rest. We have him heavily sedated so he will be out for the night. We will check on Bill in the morning. The sedation should be wearing off and he should be awake by the morning. Everyone can go home and come back tomorrow as he is going to be sleep through the night."

The doctor then asked – "does anyone have any questions?" After a brief period of silence, Bill's son David asked – "Doctor, what if there is bleeding and swelling in his head? What is done for that?"

"Good question." The doctor said. "If there is bleeding and/or swelling – depending on the severity of both, we may have to drill into his skull to relieve the pressure and stop the bleeding." Those comments were a wet blanket on everyone's feelings – after feeling pretty good about the doctor's initial report. The doctor sensed that and concluded by saying – "look, Bill pulling through surgery is an obviously a very good sign. Not many 70-year-olds would have survived the trauma that he experienced today. He has a really strong heart and a strong will to live. On a personal note - I have known Bill for a few years and if anyone has God on his side, it is him. Please go home and get some rest. You can come back in the morning."

The doctor than exited back into the OR. Everyone was standing around looking at each other not sure what to do next. Nobody wanted to leave, but that is what they were being told. At that time, Janet's phone rang. She looked at the caller ID and it was Katie. She answered –

"Katie, what is going on?"

"Janet, we have a slight problem in the lobby."

"What kind of problem?" Everyone in the waiting room turned toward Janet upon hearing the word PROBLEM. Janet asked – "by the way, what time is it? Shouldn't you be home?"

Katie responded – "Yes, but I can't leave until you see this, we need your advice."

"OK – I will be right there.

Janet turned to everyone in the waiting room and instructed them to stay there until she figured out what the problem was in the lobby. She departed the waiting room heading for the lobby.

About 10 minutes later, Rose's phone rang. She saw that it was Janet and she answered.

"Rose, please bring everyone in the waiting room out to the lobby.

Rose asked. "What is going on – what's the problem?"

"Rose, just bring everyone to the lobby and you will see."

Rose told everyone that Janet wanted all of them to go to the lobby. Rose took the long way back through the cafeteria. The hospital seemed empty, like a Sunday night. Rose assumed that it was because of the earlier lockdown.

As they approached the lobby, she could hear a buzz or rumble like a bunch of people talking. She turned the corner to the lobby and was shocked to see the lobby was full of people. There had to be 100 people or more. She saw Janet and Katie by the reception desk and headed over to them with everyone else from the waiting room following her. Meanwhile, the people in the lobby had spotted this group and all eyes were on them like they were expecting something.

Rose got to the reception desk with Bill's sons directly behind her. Rose asked – "Janet, what is this - who are these people?"

"These people - these people are some of the patients and family of patients who Bill has helped over the years. They say that they are not leaving until they know Bill is OK.

"Oh my God." Rose stated out-loud.

Rose and all the others just stood there in stunned silence and glanced across the many faces in the crowd standing in front of them. Rose noticed the young couple that she met months ago after their child had passed. There were young and old couples – many with their young children in tow. The crowded included black, white, Hispanic and Asian – the virtual UN that you hear about.

Stephanie looked at Robert with an incredulous stare. Robert knew his sister was staring at him and he didn't even turn his head to face her. He just uttered – "I know, I know."

"Janet, I can't talk to these people." Rose stated.

"Well, somebody has to." Janet answered.

With that somebody in crowd yelled – "How's Bill?" Rose turned and looked at Matthew and David. Matthew volunteered – "I will do it."

Matthew stepped forward with David right behind. He then introduced himself – someone yelled – "I can't hear you." So, Matthew started talking much louder. He introduced himself again and then his brother and Rose. He then basically repeated the update that the doctor had given them 20 minutes earlier. He stressed that he was still in critical condition and that he would be out for the night. As such, there would be no meaningful updates until the morning.

When he stated that his dad had pulled through surgery and was OK – he had to pause because there was a few minutes of applause and cheering. Matthew, thinking quickly on his feet, said that as soon as he got home, he would create a website to provide updates on his dad's condition. He said that he would name it BillDelnor.com. He thanked everyone for coming.

Janet then stepped up and stressed that everyone needed to go home as they needed to clear the lobby. The crowd started to move but not toward the exits but directly toward them. There was a brief moment of anxiety as Matthew and David weren't sure what was happening as the crowd approached. One by one the people shook their hands or gave them a hug, telling them what their dad had done or meant to them. This took some time as everyone wanted to tell their story about how Bill had helped them and emphasized how they were ready to help if any help was needed. They wanted to give Matthew and David their contact info but they stressed to just check the website and to leave their contact info there.

Again, Stephanie and Robert were steps away witnessing all of this. Stephanie again looked at Robert and again he responded – "I KNOW, I KNOW."

After everyone in the lobby had departed, the people from the waiting room all headed home. Janet, Belynda, Debbie and her parents along with Bill's sons all said their goodbyes and that they would be back tomorrow. Robert and Stephanie started to walk toward the parking garage with Rose. Rose stopped abruptly, sorry but my car is parked on the other side in the visitor lot. I will talk to you guys later or in the morning. She thanked both of them for coming. Stephanie wanted Robert to walk Rose to her car but Rose wouldn't hear of it. So, off they went to the garage and off Rose went in the opposite direction to the visitor parking lot.

Except – Rose had no intention of going home.

18 – ALL IN

Rose knew that Bill would be in recovery for a couple of hours and that there was no way she was getting into the OR to see him. However, after that, he would be going up to the ICU and she would have a chance to see him up there. Rose checked her phone and it was 7 PM. The second shift would be on duty in the ICU. She did not know the 2nd shift ICU nurses. The police were gone. There was nobody in the first-floor elevator bay to prevent her from going up to the 5th floor.

When she got to the 5th floor there was nobody around when she got off of the elevator. She then entered the 5th floor lobby which led to the ICU and cancer patient post-surgery areas. The door to those areas would certainly be locked, but Rose checked anyway. It was locked. She went to the receptionist window and looked in. She couldn't see any of the nurses and assumed that they were in their stations. She saw a doorbell type button and pushed it. She heard a buzzer go off inside, but got no response. The nurses could be busy so she waited for five minutes and then pushed it again. Again, no response. After about another five minutes a young nurse appeared at the window and asked – "can I help you?"

Rose explained who she was and that she was waiting for Bill to come up to the ICU. The nurse understood and said that that they knew Bill was coming, but didn't expect him for an hour or two. The nurse reminded Rose that the visiting hours for the ICU ended at 6 PM. As such, she would not be allowed to see Bill until tomorrow. She also stated that because of Bill's condition, he may not be allowed visitors at all. Rose decided not to fight that battle yet. "OK." She replied. "I will just wait here until I know that he is up in the ICU. Will you please let me know when he arrives." Rose asked. The nurse promised that she would and off she went.

Rose took a seat in the waiting area. She checked her phone and saw that she had a text from GG, but didn't have the desire or strength to talk to her right now. She also noticed that her phone battery was down to 8%. Crap, she said out-loud – as she realized that her charger was at home. She thought about asking the nurse if they had a charger, but then remembered that they kept one downstairs at the main lobby reception desk.

She went down and saw that Gary was manning the desk. "Rose – what are you doing here?" He asked?

"I need to use the phone charger." She reached under the desk and plugged her phone in, knowing that it would take about 30 minutes to charge.

"What a crazy day! How is Bill doing?" Gary asked?

"He is in recovery, I am waiting for him to be sent up to the ICU. Hey, do you mind watching my phone while I run to the cafeteria?"

"No problem."

Rose headed over to the cafeteria for some coffee and something to eat. She had missed both lunch and dinner. There is not much food available after 7 PM. There are just pre-packaged sandwiches, chips or cookies. Rose grabbed a coffee and some cookies and took a seat to relax for a few minutes. She thought of sitting where she normally sat with Bill, but that didn't feel right - she just took a seat near the door.

As she was enjoying a little nourishment, she noticed Janet walking through the cafeteria at a brisk pace heading somewhere. Rose called out to her and waved. Janet stopped and looked around not knowing who was calling her at first. Finally, she set eyes on Rose and started to head over.

"Janet, what are you still doing here?"

"I could ask you the same thing, Rose. I had to catch up on a few things that needed to get done before tomorrow. What about you?"

"I am waiting for Bill to be brought up to the ICU."

"Rose, you know that they are not going to let you in to see him tonight."

"I know, I was already up there and the nurses told me the same thing. Do you know the head nurse on duty tonight?"

"I do – why?"

"I was thinking that maybe you could give her a call and explain things."

"Rose, I have no authority with the nurses when it comes to medical decisions and this is a medical decision."

"I know but you never know. A call may help."

"OK, I will call her. Anything else?"

"Well, depending on how things go tonight, I may not be at the desk tomorrow."

"I know, I already told Katie that she would be on the desk again tomorrow."

"Thanks Janet."

Off Janet went at her rapid pace. Rose finished and returned to the reception desk to get her phone which was now fully charged. She headed back up to the ICU to wait for Bill.

As she got off the elevator on the 5th floor, just as before, the place looked deserted. She entered the reception area / waiting room and she was startled to see another person sitting there with their back to Rose. It was obviously a man so Rose walked to the left side of the room to take a seat and get a look at the individual. She then realized that it was Bill's son David.

"David, I am surprised to see you! I thought that you went home?"

"I started to but realized that I had to be here for my dad. If things were reversed and it was me in here, he would not be going home. He would stay with me."

"That is certainly true." Rose decided to change seats and took a seat next to David.

"What about work?" Rose asked. "Don't you have to go in tomorrow?"

"No, I texted my boss and told her that I wouldn't be coming in. She understood and told me to take a couple of days. Culligan is great that way."

It was the first time that Rose and David had been alone together. In fact, Rose had only met David twice. Once at the introduction lunch at the country club and a second time when Bill and her had met him for lunch on a Saturday. In both instances, David was cordial but distant and quiet. So, it surprised Rose when he started talking.

"You know, I am really worried about my dad. They say when something like this happens to an older person that they are never the same. I mean that they never fully recover. My God, a gunshot and a fractured skull. That would be devastating for a young person, let alone a 70-year-old. I am in my 30's and I am terrified of not having him around. I am just now getting past my mother dying. If Dad dies – I." Rose cut him off in mid-sentence feeling that David was about to lose it. She reached over and took his hand.

"David, you know better than me what a special guy your dad is. However, I know, I am confident that he is going to pull through this. It is not his time yet."

With those words from Rose, David seemed to relax a bit and sit back into his chair – still holding Rose's hand.

Bill had always been present in the past as a buffer and help carry the conversation. Now without Bill there, it was amazing how easy it was for them. There was a couple of awkward pauses when both would look at their cell phones but for the most part, they were able to carry the conversation and David never let go of Rose's hand.

Rose checked her phone and saw that it was about 8 PM and still no Bill. She was starting to get a little worried. She went back to the receptionist window and rang the bell. As she was waiting for the nurse to come to the window, the door to the ICU opened. The same nurse that Rose spoke to earlier was there standing in the doorway holding the door.

The nurse was a little surprised to see two people waiting. She asked – "I assume that both of you are waiting for news on Bill?"

Rose stepped forward. "Yes – is he up here yet?"

Yes. We just got him settled into the room. He remains in stable condition and fast asleep."

David asked – "what about the scan on his head? Did you get those results yet?"

"Yes, there was no internal bleeding and just minor swelling so no surgery is needed on his head. He almost certainly has a concussion and will have a nasty headache when he wakes up."

"Do you still plan to wake him in the morning?" Rose was glad that David was there. He was asking good detailed questions that she wasn't thinking about.

The nurse answered. "The doctor will make that determination in the morning. I really couldn't say right now.?

"Any more questions?" The nurse asked.

Rose now jumped in and made her request that she knew would be rejected. "I would really like to see him."

"Sorry." The nurse quickly replied. "No visitors in the ICU until after 9 AM tomorrow."

Rose noticed the nurses name tag. "Cindy, do you know who Bill is and who I am?"

"Yes, I do Rose. I have spent many nights with Bill here in the ICU, but he had special clearance from the hospital."

"Did Janet call you?"

"Yes, and she pushed hard for you being allowed to see Bill but I can't do it."

David jumped in. "Cindy, there must not be a medical reason that we can't see my dad because you are saying that tomorrow morning it will be OK – right?"

"That is correct. It is simply hospital policy regarding visitors to the ICU and I could get into big trouble if I let you in."

Rose then asked – "OK Cindy, what if we just make it a quick visit? Just to see him briefly." Rose realized that she had said we to include David.

"Sorry Rose. I can't do it."

Rose thought for a brief moment and thought – OK, the nice approach isn't working, so here goes nothing.

"Cindy, does the hospital have security on the 2nd shift?"

Cindy looked confused with Rose's question. "I assume so Rose. Why are you asking?"

"Because you need to call them." Rose told her.

"Why do I need security?"

"Because Cindy, I am going into Bill's room and you are not going to be able to stop me."

Cindy looked down at the door handle and realized that Rose had maneuvered over while they were talking and now had her hand firmly on the exterior side of the door handle. There was no way Cindy was going to be able to close the door.

"OK Rose. This is nuts! Please just go home and rest and come back in the morning. That will be better for everyone – including Bill."

"Cindy, you say that you know Bill – if I was laying in there or his son (as she pointed to David) was laying in there, do you think he would go home?"

Cindy looked at Rose and then at David for a while thinking about what to do and finally said – "OK. If I get fired, I am suing both of you. You both have to wash your hands and then put on masks and gowns." Rose and David did as Cindy instructed. Cindy then guided them to Bill's room. Before going in she turned to Rose and David and gave some final instructions.

"When you go in – no touching. He is very fragile. Also, he has been through an awful experience and therefore his appearance may be a little shocking and unsettling for you. You need to hold it together and keep quiet for his sake of the other patients. There is only one chair inside so one of you will have to stand. I will give you 15 minutes and then you have to leave – agreed?" Both Rose and David replied – "agreed."

The first sight of Bill was shocking. His head was heavily bandaged and his color was extremely pale. He had an IV in his left arm and a breathing tube in his mouth. They could not see his hip area due to the blankets. They could tell that this area was heavily bandaged and that his left leg was elevated. The side gates to the bed were raised as obviously, they didn't want anyone near him.

Rose immediately took a seat near the bedside. She looked around to make sure that Cindy wasn't nearby and put her hand under the gate to take a hold of Bill's right hand. David remained standing just looking at his dad. Rose could see that the sight of his dad was having an impact on David. His eyes were welling up with tears as he just stared down at his dad.

Rose wanting to comfort David stated – "David, he is going to be fine." Rose continued, "now that I have seen him, I know that he will be OK."

David shook his head in response. "I know"

The 15 minutes came and went and Cindy had not come back. After about an hour, Cindy came back in and was speaking in a very hushed voice. "OK, I have now spoken to Erin and the doctor. It is OK for you to be here, unless I am changing the bandages – which I am about to do now. However, just one person can be in here at a time." She looked at David when she said that. "So, both of you will have to leave while I check the bandages. I will let you know when I am finished. Then, one of you can come back in."

David and Rose both got up and headed for the waiting room. Rose asked about the gowns and masks. "Should we keep them?"

Cindy replied. "No - the doctor said they weren't needed so you can put those in the bin near the nurse's station."

Rose and David did as Cindy asked and opened the door back into the waiting room. Both were surprised to find Robert sitting in the room waiting for them.

"Robert, what are you doing here?" Rose asked?

"Looking for you. I waited for you at your apartment and after an hour figured that you pulled a fast one and stayed at the hospital."

"Good thinking." Rose said sheepishly.

Robert said hello to David and they shook hands. He then turned to Rose. "Mom, it has been a long day for you. You should go home and get some sleep and come back in the morning."

David agreed with Robert saying that he would stay and let Rose know if anything changed during the night.

"Great." Robert said, looking at Rose, expecting or hoping that she would agree.

Rose thought for a second and then responded. "No. I am going to stay for a while. I will be fine if you guys want to head home and get some sleep." Rose then sat down in the waiting room.

Robert then approached his mom. He took another shot at getting her to go home and get some rest. When Robert finished, Rose took his hand and looked up at him and in a definitive and firm voice said – "Robert, I am staying, end of discussion."

David then said that he was going to stay as well and took a seat. Robert then didn't say anything and took a seat next to his mother.

About 30 minutes had passed when Cindy returned to the waiting room and said that she was done and one of them could return. Rose and David looked at each other and David said – "Rose you go ahead. We can take turns whenever you are ready."

Rose said "thanks." She stood up and walked to David and gave him a kiss on the cheek. She then did the same to Robert, thanking him for being there.

Rose returned to Bill's room and again took the same seat and held his hand. After about an hour she went out to the waiting room and let David go in. They continued taking turns for the rest of the night until the doctor arrived about 7:00 AM.

David was in his father's room when he arrived and the doctor asked him to step outside while he examined Bill. After about 30 minutes, Dr.

Samuel came out to the waiting room. Rose, David and Robert stood up when he entered the waiting room. Please sit the doctor said and he took a seat next to Rose.

Bill remains stable. He has been resting for around 12 hours. His readings are a little weak, but we are going to let the sedative wear off and see if we can wake him. It could take 10 minutes to an hour for him to fully wake up. We are a little uncertain because of the blow to his head. You just never know with a head injury. Also, we have Bill on strong pain medication. Even when he wakes, he may not seem as alert as normal. One last thing, the doctor stated. Bill is likely to have no memory about what happened to him yesterday. So be prepared for that and don't feel like you need to tell him everything right away. That can be overwhelming. The nurse will come get you with he begins to wake up. The doctor then returned to the ICU.

Rose decided that she needed to hit the restroom, which was just outside of the waiting room. When she returned, Matthew had arrived and gotten an update from David on what the doctor said.

The door to the ICU then opened and a different nurse, Carol – was there saying that Bill should be waking and that they could come in. They hesitated for a brief moment as they were not sure how many could go in. The nurse jumped in saying three could go in. So, Rose, Matthew and David all headed to Bill's room.

When Matthew got into the room, he was a bit taken aback by the way his dad looked. However, he had a plan. He had brought in his dad's cell phone which he plugged into an outlet. He loaded some of this dad's favorite music and programmed the phone to play the music continuously. His dad's favorite was Legacy by Paul Reeves which was used by the JW Marriott in their promotional video that his dad had heard many times during his extensive business travels.

The doctor was standing there with the nurse and said now we just wait. Rose walked over and took Bill's hand. The doctor said watch his eye lids and hands for movement, but nothing happened.

After a few minutes, the doctor said "talk to him." Rose started and then Matthew and David joined in calling their dad, but again no response.

Matthew reached down to his plugged-in phone and turned up the volume but still nothing.

Finally, David approached the bed and leaned over the railing putting his face about six inches from this father's face and yelled – "DAD!" With that, Bill's left eye popped open and both hands moved. His right eye then opened slowly and Rose could feel Bill squeezing her hand softly.

Bill turned his head slowly looking around the room and looking briefly at each of them. For a moment they weren't sure if he recognized them. Slowly a smile came across his face and he winked his right eye.

Dr. Samuel approached Bill and introduced himself and asked him if he knew where he was, but got no response. He then asked Bill what his name was, but again no response. Bill just continued to look around the room. He then stepped to the side and asked Bill if he knew who these people were – pointing at Rose, Matthew and David. Again - no response - just a blank stare from Bill.

The doctor then started to explain to everyone that there was no reason to panic as this was normal for a person in Bill's condition. In the middle of his comments, Matthew interrupted. Matthew pointed to his dad and said – he is trying to say something. They all turned around and they could see that Bill was trying to move his lips and say something. The doctor quickly moved closer and leaned over putting his right ear next to Bill's mouth. It was dead quiet in the room as the doctor listened. Nobody else could hear what Bill was saying as he was simply too weak. The doctor stood up and faced everyone – he said "My Family".

19 – THE MERGER

It had been six months since the "incident" at Delnor. It had impacted many people and much has changed as a result.

About 18 hours after the shooting, Bill was awake. He slowly regained his strength and was able to talk but remained very weak and slept a lot. Amazingly, he remembered everything up until the time he fell and hit his head. He spent another few days in the ICU and then transferred to a regular room and then to a rehab hospital. Rose was with him every day and many nights. She would go home at least every other day to change and clean-up and grab a quick nap. Whenever she wasn't there, one or both of Bill's sons were there.

Rose's family also became frequent visitors, especially Jordan. He would spend hours with Bill talking golf and the Cubs. Jordan had become a serious fan of both. Bill had called his country club and arranged for Jordan to play the course and use the practice facilities whenever he wanted. On some days, Stephanie would drop Jordan off in the morning on the way to work and pick him up on the way home. Jordan became well known around the club. Many friends of Bill would invite Jordan to play with them. As a result, Jordan's game continued to improve.

Robert also was a regular visitor – normally during the off hours. Whenever he was there, Rose would make an excuse to leave the room so the two of them were forced to be alone. The alone time was awkward at first as they had little in common, but eventually it became deep political and social discussions. Robert was learning that there were two sides to every issue and that he couldn't believe everything that was said on CNN or MSNBC. Also, that it was OK to disagree on issues. Disagreement didn't make the other person evil.

Erin and Debbie returned to their normal duties in the ICU and both were constant visitors, caretakers and companions of Bill as well. Erin and Bill established a special bond as both had saved each other. It seemed a lot like soldiers who had come through combat together.

Belynda and Janet also made daily visits while at work. They would check on Rose to see if she needed anything, but also to check on Bill. They often would bring him something to eat that they had made at home.

The details about what happened that day in the ICU had become public and was big news in the local papers and TV shows. Bill and the hospital began receiving numerous requests for an interview with Bill but he rejected all of them. The calls into the hospital immediately after the incident about the status of Bill's condition overwhelmed the switchboard. Delnor started referring people to the BillDelnor website that Matthew had created and slowly the calls diminished.

Bill also had to endure a police investigation around the shooting. Even though it was pretty much an open and shut case, it required a formal investigation because it was classified as a homicide. Bill, Erin and Debbie were interviewed numerous times about what happened in the ICU room on that day. Both local police and the Kane County Sheriff were involved in taking the interviews, as well as, the DA for both communities. It was finally ruled a justifiable homicide by a grand jury. Bill, Erin and Debbie all had to testify and all three told consistent stories. Bill's testimony was taped from his hospital room.

During this legal process the county sheriff had arranged a protective watch to be place around Bill's home. There was a concern that the prisoner's family, friends or associates could attempt to seek revenge on Bill. The sheriff arranged almost hourly drive byes on Bill's house and would frequently park a car on his street just to show a presence. After about 3 months, there was no sign of any interest or threat and the county pulled the protective watch.

The city of Geneva and Kane County had both approached Bill about having a special ceremony at which they would present Bill with an award for his heroism and service. Bill flatly rejected both saying that he was not a hero.

After two weeks in the rehab facility, Bill got to go home. Rose quit her job at Delnor and was staying full time at Bill's house taking care of him. He had two more surgeries to clean up the injuries from the bullet to his hip. Each time it was a few days in the hospital and a few more days of recovery back at home. Rose was the rock through all of this. Bill seemed to get stronger each day. He was now only dependent on a cane, but knew that his golf days were probably over.

The shooting had been a horrible day for many people and for the hospital. However, in the end, it had dramatically changed Bill and Rose's family dynamic.

Rose was now living at Bill's house, because taking care of him has been a full-time job. She still had her apartment, but the lease was expiring soon. Bill had been paying the rent because Rose had to quit her job at Delnor to stay with him. Rose had pretty much dropped all of her friends as she was tired of having to justify her relationship with Bill. She still talked or texted with GG, but it was just not the same.

Sundays had now become a special day for Bill and Rose. They would cook or grill a meal for whomever could come and it was always served at 3 PM. The regulars were always Matthew and David and their families and Stephanie and Robert and their families, which was about 10 people including Bill and Rose. In addition, on many Sundays, Erin and her family would participate, Debbie and her parents, and occasionally Belynda and Janet would also stop by with their families. In total it was almost 23 people, if everyone attended. A lot of work for Bill and Rose, but they loved it and everyone attending seemed to enjoy it as well.

A side benefit occurred when David and Debbie started dating. Rose had thought that she noticed something between them during David's visits to the ICU to see his dad. Now their relationship was public knowledge and Rose and Bill couldn't be happier.

Today is a special day for Bill and Rose. He has an appointment with his surgeon Dr. Samuel at Delnor at 11:30 AM. This should be his last check up from his injury and the several surgeries that he has undergone. Bill has made reservations at Hugo's Frog Bar in Naperville for 1:00 PM so he and Rose can celebrate being done with all of the medical issues.

Bill and Rose arrived about 30 minutes early for Bill's appointment, which was normal for Bill as he is paranoid about being late. Bill also believed that the earlier you arrived – the earlier you departed. They checked in with the receptionist upon arrival and were told that Dr. Samuel had not arrived yet, but that they expected him shortly. There was one other patient waiting ahead of Bill, which he assumed was there for an 11 AM appointment time.

At about 11:25, the receptionist came out of the door and informed everyone waiting – which was still only Bill and Rose and the one other patient – that the doctor just called and was running late due to an emergency. She said that it could be another 30 to 60 minutes before he arrives. She suggested that they go down to the cafeteria and that she would text them as soon as he arrived.

The other patient agreed and gave the receptionist his cell number so she could text him. Bill turned to Rose and asked her if they should wait or re-schedule the appointment for another day. Rose quickly replied that they should wait and get the appointment and final check-up done today. Bill agreed and gave the receptionist his cell number and then they headed down to the cafeteria.

They got down to the first floor and then proceeded to the cafeteria. They walked past the reception desk on the way. Rose had expected to see Belynda at the desk but instead there was a new attendant and her name was Karen. Rose did not know her because she had been hired since Rose left. Rose stopped at the desk anyway and introduced herself and Bill. Karen was excited to meet both of them saying that she had heard a lot about both of them.

As they approached the cafeteria Bill mentioned to Rose that they hadn't been back in the cafeteria for some time. He also mentioned that it was kind of their special place – where they first sat down and got to know each other. Rose smiled and agreed – that it is a special place. This brief back and forth kept them from noticing a low murmur of people talking that appeared to be coming from the cafeteria.

As they entered the cafeteria and looked to the right where their normal seats were, they were stunned. Around their favorite table was a group of maybe 50 people, who were applauding and cheering their arrival. Bill took Rose's hand as they walked toward their table. Rose turned to Bill and asked – "what is this?"

"I have no idea." Bill replied. He just kept walking and holding Rose's hand.

Bill and Rose noticed that everyone was there. Present were Bill's sons, Rose's children and grandchildren, Erin, Debbie, Janet and Belynda and many other people from Delnor – including Dr. Samuel and the cafeteria ladies.

When they arrived at the table, they noticed that their lunches were already there. A turkey sandwich for Bill and a soup and salad for Rose.

Rose tried to ask what was going on and attempted to hug everyone, but her daughter grabbed her arm and told her to just sit down and eat. Rose was embarrassed – not understanding what was happening. Bill held the chair for Rose as she sat down and then walked around the table to take his seat. However, he stopped before sitting and reached into his coat pocket.

The room got quiet as Bill held his hand up, showing a ring box to everyone. He turned to Rose and started speaking.

"Rose Hopkins, I have been in love with you since our first lunch in this cafeteria in these very chairs. We have endured a few challenges and obstacles over our brief time together, but our love has carried us through those issues. Over the past six months you have been my rock and I simply would not have made it without you. I am sorry that I can't get down on one knee, but would you accept this ring and do me the honor of marrying me?"

Rose had been listening with her hands over her mouth in shock. The tears were flowing down her face and she immediately stood and said "absolutely I will." With that she hugged Bill and a loud cheer erupted from the gathering.

The cafeteria crew served champagne to everyone as there were hugs, kisses and tears from everyone.

One month later, Bill and Rose would get married in a civil ceremony at his house on a Sunday during one of their weekly gatherings at 3 PM. It was attended by the usual crowd, plus a few extras or a total of about 30 people.

20 – LEAVING A MARK

French Lick is a small town in southern Indiana about one hour south of Indiana University which is in Bloomington, IN. French Lick has been a resort town since the mid 1800's with the discovery of natural sulfur springs, which were believed to have healing properties. A number of famous people have visited the area over the years including Franklin Roosevelt, who announced his intention to run for president at the French Lick Springs Hotel.

More recently, French Lick had become a golf resort region with the construction of two championship level courses by famous golf architects, Donald Ross and Pete Dye.

In early May of this year a little over 10 years after the incident at Delnor, French Lick is hosting the Big Ten Conference Men's Golf Championship. It is the last day of the four-day event with both the team and individual titles to be decided. Indiana held a two-stroke lead over Illinois at the start of today's final round for the team championship and Brian Greco (IL) held a three-stroke lead over Jordan Tucker (IN).

By the time the final twosome reached the 18th tee, Indiana had secured the team championship by 5 strokes. It was Indiana's third consecutive Big Ten Golf Championship and Jordan had tied Brian for the individual championship. Therefore, the winner of the 18th hole would be the champion, unless they tied and had to go to a sudden death playoff.

The 18th hole on the Pete Dye course was a long par 5 at 626 yards. Both players were about 100 yards short of the green after their second shots and both were in the fairway. The both hit good wedge shots, Brian to about 20 feet from the hole and Jordan just inside of him at about 18 feet. Brian putted first. His putt just slid past the left edge of the hole to about 10 inches past the hole. Jordan now had an opportunity to win the hole and the Big Ten Championship individual honors if the made his putt.

Jordan had just recently graduated from Indiana with an Accounting Degree and 3.5 GPA. He had a job offer from Deloitte in Chicago, who he had interned with during the last two summers. He was also considering taking a shot at the PGA tour. He knew that making a go at professional golf would be a challenge, but he was leaning in that direction right now.

Jordan lined up his putt and looked ready to hit it, but then backed off and looked at the putt again. He was obviously nervous as he normally played quickly, but now appeared to be stalling a bit while reading the putt again. He then stopped and looked skyward and closed his eyes. After about 15 seconds he returned to earth and approached his putt. He took his stance and made a confident and solid stroke. The putt had a left to right break. The speed was perfect, as was the line and the ball dropped directly into the hole.

The cheers exploded from both the audience and his team mates. Jordan raised his hands in celebration. He removed his hat and shook his opponent's hand. He was then mobbed by his teammates as they celebrated his victory as this years Big Ten Golf Champion! As he walked off the green with his teammates, he stopped and looked for his family. He saw them waiting at the side of the green and turned and made a beeline directly to them.

When he reached them a second and more emotional celebration took place. He was greeted by his parents and sister, his uncle Robert with his wife and two kids, Matthew with his wife and two kids, David and Debbie with their son – 13 people in total. All engaged in a group hug with Jordan in the center. Tears were flowing and Jordan again raised his hand pointing to the sky and looked up with closed eyes out of respect.

Remaining at the side of the green was Jordan's IU bright red golf bag. It was standing alone in a stream of sunlight from setting sun like an observer of the emotional family gathering. The bag had HOOSIERS in bright white lettering on the side facing away from the group. On the side facing Jordan and his family – written in script – was – ***Mr. Bill and Grandma Rose***.

They had the best seat in the house.

HAPPY B-DAY — MARTHA

L. HENDRICK